Tenth Edition

Pennsylvania
NOTARY PRIMER

The NNA's Handbook
for Pennsylvania Notaries

NATIONAL NOTARY ASSOCIATION

Published by
National Notary Association
9350 De Soto Avenue
Chatsworth, CA 91311-4926
Phone: (800) 876-6827
Fax: (818) 700-0920
Website: NationalNotary.org
Email: nna@nationalnotary.org

©2019 National Notary Association
ALL RIGHTS RESERVED. No part of this book may be reproduced in any form without permission in writing from the publisher.

The information in this *Primer* is correct and current at the time of its publication, although new laws, regulations and rulings may subsequently affect the validity of certain sections. This information is provided to aid comprehension of state Notary Public requirements and should not be construed as legal advice. Please consult an attorney for inquiries relating to legal matters.

Tenth Edition, Second Printing ©2019
First Edition ©2001

ISBN: 978-1-59767-247-4

Table of Contents

Introduction 1

The Notary Appointment 2

Screening the Signer 10

Reviewing the Document 16

Common Notary Acts 23

Notary Journal 35

Notary Certificate 39

Notary Stamp 43

Electronic Notarization 46

Prohibited Actions & Administrative Penalties 50

Pennsylvania Laws Pertaining to Notaries Public 54

About the NNA 109

Index 110

Have a Tough Notary Question?

If you were a National Notary Association member, you could get the answer to that difficult question. Join the NNA® and your membership includes access to the NNA® Hotline* and live Notary experts providing the latest Notary information regarding laws, rules and regulations.

Hours
Monday–Friday   5:00 a.m.–7:00 p.m. (PT)
Saturdays   5:00 a.m.–5:00 p.m. (PT)

NNA® Hotline Toll-Free Phone Number: 1-888-876-0827

After hours you can leave a message or email our experts at Hotline@NationalNotary.org and they will respond the next business day.

*Access to the NNA® Hotline is for National Notary Association members and NNA® Hotline subscribers only. Call and become a member today.

Introduction

The *Pennsylvania Notary Primer* provides you with a resource to help decipher the many laws and regulations that affect notarization. This resource takes you through the important aspects of Pennsylvania's Notary laws, regulations and best practices, and puts them in easy-to-understand terms.

For your convenience, we have reprinted the complete text of the laws of Pennsylvania that relate to Notaries, some of which went into effect in the fall of 2017. Whether you're about to be appointed for the first time or are a longtime Notary, we're sure that the *Pennsylvania Notary Primer* will provide you with new insight and understanding of your official duties.

Most Notary laws and recommendations can be found in the Pennsylvania Statutes (PS) or the Department of State's website: Pennsylvania Department of State website (Dos.pa.gov).

For step-by-step instructions on the commission application process, applicants may also visit: Nationalnotary.org.

                           Milton G. Valera
                           Chairman
                           National Notary Association

The Notary Appointment

Qualification for Appointment

Qualifications. To become a Notary Public in Pennsylvania, the applicant must meet the following requirements (57 Pa.C.S.A. 321[a]):

- Be at least 18 years of age.

- Be a citizen or permanent legal resident of the United States.

- Be a resident of or have a place of employment or practice in the Commonwealth of Pennsylvania.

- Be able to read and write English.

- Not have committed an act or omission which demonstrates a lack of honesty, integrity, competence or reliability.

- Complete three hours of approved Notary education.

- Pass an approved examination.

Application Submission

Application. An online application is available on the Department of State's website (*Notaryreg.pa.gov*) for all new and renewing Notaries.

Required Documentation. Proof of completing the required education must be submitted with the application. Also, if applicable, documentation and an explanation for criminal history,

Notary disciplinary action and/or any professional occupational license disciplinary action must be submitted with the application.

Application Fee. The application fee is $42 for both first-time and renewing applicants. This amount includes the application for Notary Public commission and a fee for filing of the bond with the Department of State (57 Pa. C.S. 321[b][2]).

Nonresident Applicants. Nonresidents may apply for a Notary commission if they have a place of employment or practice in Pennsylvania (57 Pa.C.S. 321[a]).

Grounds for Denial

The Department may deny an application for reasons that include any of the following (57 Pa.C.S. 323.a):

- An act or omission which demonstrates a lack of honesty, integrity, competence or reliability as a Notary.

- A fraudulent, dishonest, or deceitful misstatement or omission of required information on an application.

- Denial, refusal to renew, revocation, suspension or conditioning of a Notary Public commission in another state.

Training and Examination

Mandatory Notary Training for New Applicants. Applicants for a Notary appointment, within the six-month period prior to application submission, are required to complete a course of at least three hours of Notary Public basic education approved by the Department. The course must either be online training or classroom instruction (57 Pa.C.S. 322.b[1-2]).

Renewing Appointment. Applicants for a renewal Notary appointment, within the six-month period prior to application submission, are required to complete a course of at least three hours of Notary Public continuing education approved by the Department. The course must either be online training or classroom instruction (57 Pa.C.S. 322.b[1-2]).

Proof of Education Completion. All applicants who successfully complete an approved course of study shall be issued a Certificate of Education by their education provider. A copy of this certificate must be submitted with the Notary's application.

Examination Requirement for New Notaries. Applicants for a new Notary commission, or those applicants that have a lapse in their commission, must pass an examination administered by the Department or an entity approved by the Department. An applicant must score 80% or better to pass the exam. An applicant can retake the exam within a six-month period as many times as necessary to pass. Exam results are valid for one year from the date of the exam. Renewing Notaries are not required to take an exam as long as the Department receives the renewal application prior to expiration of the current commission (57 Pa. C.S. 322[a]).

Notary Bond

Requirement. Every Pennsylvania Notary is required to obtain a surety bond in the amount of $10,000 and record it with the office of the county Recorder of Deeds within 45 days after appointment (57 Pa. C.S. 321[d]).

The Notary bond must be executed by an insurance company authorized to do business in the Commonwealth of Pennsylvania (57 Pa. C.S. 321[d][3][i]).

Purpose. The Notary bond protects the public, not the Notary, from a Notary's misconduct or negligence. The bond provides coverage for damages to anyone who suffers financially from a Notary's actions — intentional or not. The surety company will seek compensation from the Notary for any damages it has to pay out on the Notary's behalf.

Filing the Bond. Once the bond has been recorded with the county Recorder of Deeds, a copy of the bond and oath of office must be filed with the Department of State within 90 days (57 Pa. C.S. 321[d][2][1-3]).

Errors and Omissions Insurance

Protects the Notary. Notaries may choose to purchase insurance to cover any unintentional errors or omissions they may make. In the event of a claim or civil lawsuit, the insurance company will provide and pay for the Notary's legal counsel and absorb any damages levied by a court or agreed to in a settlement, up to the policy coverage limit. Generally, errors and omissions insurance does not cover the Notary for dishonest, fraudulent or criminal acts or omissions, or for willful or intentional disregard of the law.

Reasonable Care

Definition. In general, reasonable care is that degree of concern and attentiveness that a person of normal intelligence and responsibility would exhibit. Complying with all pertinent laws is the first rule of reasonable care for a Notary. If there are no clear statutory guidelines in a given instance, then the Notary should go to extremes to use the common sense and prudence that comprise reasonable care. If a Notary fails to do so, he or she may be subject to a civil lawsuit to recover financial damages caused by the Notary's error. However, in the event of a civil suit, if a Notary can show to a judge or jury that he or she did everything expected of a reasonable person, the judge or jury is obligated by law to find the Notary not liable for damages.

Filing Oath of Office and Signature

Requirement. Upon appointment and before issuance of a Notary commission, an applicant must execute an oath or affirmation of office with the county Recorder of Deeds in the county where the Notary will maintain an office within 45 days after appointment. A Notary cannot execute his or her own oath (57 Pa. C.S. 321[c]).

The oath appears on page two of the Notary bond that is mailed from the Secretary of the Commonwealth once the Notary's appointment application has been approved.

Registering Signature. The Notary must register his or her signature with the prothonotary in the county where the Notary maintains an office within 45 days of appointment. In counties of the second class (between 500,000 and 1,500,000 in population), the Notary must register his or her signature with the clerk of court's office (57 Pa. C.S. 321[d][7][1-2]).

Appointment of Commission

Issuance of Commission Certificate. Upon determination that an applicant has complied with all requirements, the Department will appoint or reappoint the applicant to the office of Notary Public and issue a commission certificate. The Department will send the commission certificate to the Recorder of Deeds of the county where the Notary maintains an office. Within 45 days after appointment and before issuance of a commission as a Notary Public, the applicant must obtain a surety bond (57 Pa. C.S. 321[d.1][1][ii][2]).

Jurisdiction

Statewide. Notaries may perform official acts throughout Pennsylvania but not beyond the Commonwealth's borders. A Notary may not witness a signing outside Pennsylvania and then return to the state to perform the notarization. All parts of a notarial act must be performed at the same time and place within the Commonwealth.

Term of Office

Four-Year Term. A Pennsylvania Notary Public's term of office is four years (57 Pa. C.S. 321[e]), ending at midnight on the commission expiration date.

Change of Address

Notify Department of State. A Notary must notify the Department within 30 days of any change in the information on file with the Department, including the notary public's office address or home address.

Notice of a change in address must be made in writing or by email and must state the effective date of the change. The Department has developed a Change of Address form to assist notaries to comply.

RULONA requires that the Notary register his or her official signature in the prothonotary's office of the county where the Notary maintains an office. Where a notary public moves the notary's office address to a different county, the Notary must register the Notary's official signature in the prothonotary's office of the new county within 30 days of moving into the new county.

Note: To change your address with the Secretary of the Commonwealth, you must use one of the approved forms below (forms available on the Secretary of State website).

Change of Name

Notify Department of State. A Notary must notify the Department within 30 days of any change in the information on file with the Department, including the Notary's legal name.

Notice of a change in name must be on a form prescribed by the Department and accompanied by evidence of the name change (such as a marriage certificate, court order or divorce decree).

Following notification to the Department, the Notary may use the new name or continue to perform notarial acts in the name in which the Notary was commissioned until the expiration of the notary's term. However, before using the new name on notarial work, the Notary public must register the new signature with the prothonotary's office of the county where the notary's office address is located and purchase a new rubber stamp seal. Application for reappointment must be made in the new name.

NOTE: To change your name with the Secretary of the Commonwealth, you must use one of the approved forms (available on the Secretary of State website).

Resignation

Procedure. Notaries public may voluntarily resign from the duties of office at any time during the course of the notary commission. Additionally, if a notary public neither resides nor works in the Commonwealth, that notary public shall be deemed to have resigned from the office of notary public as of the date the residency ceases or employment within the Commonwealth terminates. A notary public who resigns his or her commission shall notify the Department of State in writing within 30 days of the effective date of the resignation, using the form below. Resigning notaries should include the notary public's name as commissioned and the effective date of the resignation. This includes notaries public who resign by virtue of removing their residence or employment from the Commonwealth. Notaries who are simply letting their commissions expire at the end of their term and do not intend to renew for another four-year term should NOT file this or any other form with the Department.

Resigning notaries public, as well as those whose commissions have expired or been revoked, pursuant to 57 Pa.C.S. § 319(e), must deliver their journal to the office of the recorder of deeds in the county where the notary public last maintained an office within 30 days of:

1) expiration of the commission of the notary public, unless the notary public applies for a commission within that time period;

2) resignation of the commission of the notary public.

Resigning notaries public, pursuant as well as those whose commissions have expired, pursuant to 57 Pa.C.S. § 318(a)(2), must disable their stamping device (notary seal) by destroying, defacing, damaging, erasing or securing it against use in a manner which renders it unusable. DO NOT send the rubber stamp seal or embosser to the Department of State. (Forms available on the Secretary of State website).

The Notary Public must also destroy the official Notary stamp and deliver the journal to the office of the Recorder of Deeds in the county where the Notary last maintained an office within 30 days of resignation (57 Pa. C.S. 318[a][2]; 57 Pa. C.S. 319[e]).

Death of Notary

Notification of death of a Notary Public should be mailed to:

> Department of State
> Bureau of Commissions, Elections and Legislation
> 210 North Office Building
> Harrisburg, PA 17120-0029

On the death or adjudication of incompetency of a current or former Notary Public, the personal representative or guardian of the Notary or a person knowingly in possession of the journal of the Notary shall deliver it within 30 days to the office of the recorder of deeds in the county where the Notary last maintained an office.

On the death or adjudication of incompetency of a Notary, the personal representative or guardian of the Notary or any person knowingly in possession of the stamping device must render it unusable by destroying, defacing, damaging, erasing or securing it against use in a manner which renders it unusable. DO NOT send the rubber stamp seal or embosser to the Department of State, Bureau of Commissions, Elections and Legislation.

Employer-Notary Agreement

Fees. The fee for a Notary Public:

1) shall be the property of the Notary; and

2) unless mutually agreed by the Notary and the employer, shall not belong to or be received by the entity that employs the Notary Public (57 Pa. C.S. 329.1 [d]).

Public Official. Notaries are appointed by the state of Pennsylvania to serve the general public, even when their appointment fee, stamp and Notary supplies are paid for by a private employer. Since the Notary's appointment belongs to the Notary, a Notary's employer may not prohibit the Notary from notarizing away from work, even if the employer paid for the Notary's appointment and supplies. ■

Screening the Signer

Personal Appearance

Requirement. The person requesting notarization must personally appear before the Notary at the time of the notarization. This means that the Notary and the signer must both be physically present, face to face in the same room, when the notarization takes place. Notarizations may never be performed over the telephone (57 Pa. C.S. 306).

Direct Communication

Requirement. The Notary must be able to communicate directly with the individual for whom a notarial act is being performed in a language they both understand, or indirectly through an interpreter who is physically present at the time of notarization and who communicates directly with the signer and the Notary in a language the interpreter understands.

Willingness

Confirmation. The Notary should make every effort to confirm that the signer is acting willingly. To confirm willingness, the Notary need only ask document signers if they are signing of their own free will. If a signer does or says anything that makes the Notary think the signer is being pressured to sign, the Notary should refuse to notarize (57 Pa. C.S. 308[a][2]).

Awareness

Confirmation. The Notary should make every effort to confirm that the signer is generally aware of what is taking place. To confirm awareness, the Notary simply makes a layperson's judgment about the signer's ability to understand what is happening. A document signer who cannot respond intelligibly in a simple conversation with the Notary should not be considered sufficiently aware to sign at that moment. If the notarization is taking place in a medical environment, the signer's doctor can be consulted for a professional opinion. Otherwise, if the signer's awareness is in doubt, the Notary should refuse to notarize (57 Pa. C.S. 308[a][1]).

Identifying Document Signers

Requirement. Under Pennsylvania law, every individual whose signature is notarized and/or who is administered an oath or affirmation by a Notary must be positively identified by the Notary. Statute prescribes three acceptable methods of identification (57 Pa. C.S. 307[a-c]):

1) The Notary's *personal knowledge* of the signer's identity.

2) Reliable *identification documents* or ID cards (see page 12).

3) The oath or affirmation of a personally known *credible identifying witness*.

Personal Knowledge of Identity

Definition. The safest and most reliable method of identifying a document signer is for the Notary to depend upon his or her own personal knowledge of the signer's identity. Personal knowledge means the Notary knows the identity of a person through dealings sufficient to provide reasonable certainty that the person has the identity claimed (57 Pa. C.S. 307[a]).

Practice Common Sense. Pennsylvania law does not specify how long a Notary must be acquainted with an individual before the Notary can claim personal knowledge of that individual's identity.

That being the case, the Notary's common sense must prevail. In general, the longer the Notary is acquainted with a person and the more interactions the Notary has had with that person, the more likely it is that the Notary can claim that he or she personally knows the individual. Whenever the Notary has a reasonable doubt about a signer's identity, that individual should not be considered personally known. Identification in such cases should be made through either a credible identifying witness or reliable identification documents.

Identification Documents (ID Cards)

Acceptable Identification Documents. A Notary may accept current identification documents from the list below as satisfactory evidence of a document signer's identity (57 Pa. C.S. 307[b]):

- U.S. passport or passport card.

- Foreign passport (providing the Notary can read and understand it).

- Driver's license or non-driver ID card issued by a U.S. state.

- Driver's license or non-driver ID card issued by Canada or Mexico (providing the Notary can read and understand it).

- Other form of government identification providing it is current and contains a signature or photograph.

Discretion. A Notary may require additional information or identification to assure the identity of the individual (57 Pa. C.S. 307[b][2][c]).

Unacceptable Identification Documents. Examples include: Birth certificates, while issued by the government, do not bear a photograph or signature of the individual named in it. Credit cards, while they bear signatures and may contain a photograph of the individual, are not issued by the government.

Fraudulent Identification. Phony ID cards are common. The Notary should scrutinize each card to ensure it is genuine and that it has not been altered by an impostor.
Some clues that an ID card may have been fraudulently altered include the following: mismatched type styles; a photograph raised from the surface; a signature that does not match the signature on the document; unauthorized lamination; and smudges, erasures, smears and discolorations.

Credible Identifying Witness

Purpose. When a document signer is not personally known to the Notary and is not able to present a reliable ID card, that signer may be identified on the oath or affirmation of a credible identifying witness (57 Pa. C.S. 307[b][2]).

SCREENING THE SIGNER

Qualifications. Pennsylvania law requires that a credible identifying witness be present at the time of the notarization, be personally known to both the Notary and the signer and swear or affirm to the Notary that the signer is the person whom the signer claims to be (57 Pa. C.S. 307[b][2]).

Credible Witness Requirements. Pennsylvania's requirements for credible identifying witnesses create a chain of personal knowledge from the Notary through the witness to the signer. Therefore, the credible identifying witness must personally know the Notary as well as the document signer (57 Pa. C.S. 307[b][2]).

Oath or Affirmation for Credible Identifying Witness. Pennsylvania Notaries should administer an oath or affirmation to the credible identifying witness. The credible identifying witness should swear or affirm that the following is true:

- The individual appearing before the Notary is the person named in the document.

- The credible witness personally knows the signer.

- The credible witness believes it would be very difficult or impossible for the signer to obtain another form of ID.

- The signer does not possess an authorized ID card.

- The credible witness does not have a direct or financial interest in the record being notarized.

Journal Entry. A brief description stating a credible witness was used for identification should be noted in the journal. A prudent Notary will also print the name and address of the credible witness in the journal.

SPECIAL CIRCUMSTANCES

Signature by Mark or Stamp

Use of Mark as Signature. Although specific notarial procedures are lacking in statute, tradition and generally accepted practice permit a person who cannot sign his or her name because of illiteracy or a physical disability to instead affix a mark — an "X" for example — as a signature, as long as there are witnesses to the making of the mark.

Witnesses. For a mark to be notarized, there should be two witnesses to the making of the mark in addition to the Notary. Both witnesses should sign the document and the Notary's journal. One witness should print legibly the marker's name beside the mark on the document, and also in the journal.

Signature-by-Mark Certificate. A properly witnessed mark is considered a valid signature under law, so no special Notary certificate is required.

Notarization Procedures. Because a properly witnessed mark is regarded as a signature by custom and law, the Notary otherwise uses no special procedures for notarizing when a signer uses a mark in lieu of a signature. The marker must personally appear before the Notary, be positively identified and fulfill any other requirements of the notarial act being performed.

Notarizing for Minors

Under Age 18. Generally, persons must reach the age of majority before they can handle their own legal affairs and sign documents for themselves. In Pennsylvania, the age of majority is 18.

Normally, parents or court-appointed guardians will sign on a minor's behalf. In certain cases, minors may lawfully sign documents and have their signatures notarized — emancipated minors engaged in business transactions or children involved as court witnesses, for example.

Include Age Next to Signature. When notarizing for a minor, the Notary should ask the young signer to write his or her age next to the signature to alert any person relying on the document that the signer is a minor. The Notary is not required to verify the minor signer's age.

Identification. The method for identifying a minor is the same as that for an adult. If the minor does not have an acceptable ID, then the other methods of identifying signers must be used, either the Notary's personal knowledge of the minor or the oath of a credible identifying witness who can identify the minor.

Refusal of Service

Discrimination. A Notary Public may not refuse to provide notarial services on the basis of a customer's race, color, national origin, religion, sexual orientation, gender identity (including pregnancy), disability or marital status.

<u>Grounds to Refuse Service</u>. A notarial officer may refuse to perform a notarial act if the notarial officer is not satisfied that:

1) the individual executing the record is competent or has the capacity to execute the record;

2) the individual's signature is knowingly and voluntarily made;

3) the individual's signature on the record or statement substantially conforms to the signature on a form of identification used to determine the identity of the individual; or

4) the physical appearance of the individual signing the record or statement substantially conforms to the photograph on a form of identification used to determine the identity of the individual (57 Pa.C.S.308[a]).

<u>General Grounds</u>. A notarial officer may refuse to perform a notarial act unless refusal is prohibited by law other than [57 Pa.C.S. Chapter 3] (57 Pa.C.S. 308[b]). ■

Reviewing the Document

Document Content

Type of Notarial Act. When looking over the document the signer has presented to be notarized, the Notary Public should examine the certificate wording to determine what type of notarial act to perform. The certificate wording is generally at the bottom of the document, just below the signature line of the document. Once the act is determined, the Notary will know how to proceed.

Missing or Unacceptable Certificate Wording. If there is no certificate wording, or if the Notary determines the wording to be unacceptable, the signer will have to direct the Notary to perform the type of notarial act of the signer's choosing. In most cases, the signer will not know what type of act is needed for the document, so he or she will need to contact the receiving agency (where the document is going), issuing agency (where the document came from), or an attorney for advice. Once the signer has identified the type of act that's needed, the Notary may attach the correct certificate form. It is important to note that the Notary is not allowed to choose, direct, or advise on what type of notarial act is needed.

Photocopies & Faxed Documents. A photocopy or faxed copy of a document may be notarized, however, the signatures on the documents presented for notarization must always be signed with a handwritten, original signature. A photocopied or faxed signature may never be notarized.

Public recorders sometimes will not accept notarized photocopies or faxes because the text of the document may be too faint to adequately reproduce in microfilming.

REVIEWING THE DOCUMENT

Incomplete Documents

Incomplete Documents. A Pennsylvania Notary may not perform a notarial act on a document that contains blank spaces or is missing the original signature of the person requesting the notarization.

Any blank spaces in a document should be filled in by the signer prior to notarization. If the blanks are inapplicable and intended to be left unfilled, the signer should line through each space or write "Not Applicable" or "N/A." The Notary may not, however, tell the signer what to write in the blanks. If the signer is unsure on how to fill the blanks, he or she should contact the document's issuer, its eventual recipient, or an attorney.

Disqualifying Interest

Principal to the Document. A Notary may not notarize his or her own signature.

Financial or Beneficial Interest. A Notary may not notarize a document in which he/she has a direct or pecuniary interest in the transaction which the Notarial Officer or the Notarial Officer's spouse has a direct or pecuniary interest. (57 Pa.C.S. 304[b][1]).

Exception. The following circumstances do not constitute a direct or financial interest (57 Pa. C.S. 304[b][2][i-iii]):

1) Being a shareholder in a publicly traded company that is a party to the notarized transaction;

2) Being an officer, director or employee of a company that is a party to the notarized transaction, unless the director, officer or employee personally benefits from the transaction or is receiving a fee that is not contingent on the completion of the notarized transaction.

Powers of Attorney. Effective January 1, 2015, Notaries may not take the acknowledgment of a power of attorney if they are named as an agent in or are a witness to the signing of that power of attorney (20 Pa.C.S. 5601[b][3]).

Relatives. A Notary may not notarize the signature of his or her spouse (57 Pa.C.S. 304[b][1]).

Although Pennsylvania state law does not expressly prohibit

notarizing for other family members, family matters may involve financial benefit in ways not easily determined at the time of notarization.

Notarizing for family members also may test the Notary's ability to act impartially. For example, a Notary who is asked to notarize a contract signed by his or her brother might attempt to persuade him to sign or not sign. A sibling is entitled to exert influence, but this is entirely improper for a Notary.

Even if a Notary has no financial interest in the document and does not attempt to influence the signer, notarizing for a relative could subject the document to a legal challenge if other parties to the transaction allege the Notary could not have acted impartially.

SPECIAL CIRCUMSTANCES WITH DOCUMENTS

I-9 Forms

I-9 Forms. The Department of State has been asked whether a notary public may complete Section 2 of the federal I-9 Employment Eligibility Verification forms…. However, the completion of Section 2 is NOT a notarial act and must not be completed under a notarial seal…. The I-9 form does not request or require any notarial act. It requires an unsworn certification from the employer or the agent of the employer. It should be clear that while a Notary may sign on behalf of an employer, the Notary does not do so in the capacity of a Notary Public under the Notary Public Law but rather as an agent of the employer. Thus, the Notary may convey that he or she is an agent for the employer in the 'Title of Employer or Authorized Representative' box in Section 2 of the I-9. However, no Notary title or seal should be used to complete the I-9 as an authorized representative of the employer (website, "Pennsylvania Notaries and Completion of I-9 Forms"; revised October 2017).

Foreign Language Documents

Foreign Language Documents. Ideally, documents in foreign languages should be referred to Pennsylvania Notaries who read and write those languages. If not available in the immediate vicinity, bilingual Notaries may often be found in foreign consulates.

Pennsylvania law does not directly address notarizing documents written in a language the Notary cannot read, however, the certificate of notarial act should be worded and completed in a language the Notary understands. Although notarizing such documents is not expressly prohibited, there are difficulties and dangers in notarizing any document the Notary cannot read. For example, Pennsylvania Notaries are required by law to record the type or title of the document in their journal, and trying to extract that information from a document that the Notary cannot read may be difficult if not impossible. However, if the information on the document is in a language the Notary can read and understand (i.e. title of document, notarial wording), the Notary can complete the act.

Foreign Language Advertising

<u>Advertisement in Languages Other Than English</u>. If a Notary Public advertises or represents that he or she offers notarial services in a language other than English, whether orally or in a record, including broadcast media, print media and the internet, the Notary Public shall include the following statement, or an alternate statement authorized or required by the Department, in the advertisement or representation, prominently and in each language used in the advertisement or representation (57 Pa. C.S. 325[d][1][c]):

> I am not an attorney licensed to practice law in this Commonwealth. I am not allowed to draft legal records, give advice on legal matters, including immigration, or charge a fee for those activities (57 Pa. C.S. 325[d]).

- A non-attorney Notary must not use the terms *"notario,"* *"notario publico"* or an equivalent non-English term. This provision applies to both English and non-English forms of communication used to advertise the Notary's services, including but not limited to business cards, stationery and signage (57 Pa. C.S. 325[c][1]).

- If the form of advertisement or representation is not broadcast media, print media or on the internet and does not permit inclusion of the statement required by this subsection because of size, it shall be displayed prominently or provided at the place of performance of the notarial act before the notarial act is performed (57 Pa. C.S. 325[d][1][c][iii]).

Wills

<u>Do Not Give Advice</u>. People often attempt to draw up wills

on their own without the benefit of legal counsel and then bring these homemade testaments to a Notary to have them "legalized," expecting the Notary to know how to proceed. In advising or assisting such persons, the Notary risks prosecution for the unauthorized practice of law. The Notary's ill-informed advice may do considerable damage to the affairs of the signer and subject the Notary to a civil lawsuit to recover losses.

Do Not Proceed Without Certificate Wording. A Notary should notarize a will only if clear instructions and a Notary certificate for each signer are provided or stipulated and if the signers are not asking questions about how to proceed. Any such questions must be answered by an attorney. Wills are highly sensitive documents, the format of which is strictly dictated by law. The slightest deviation from these laws can nullify a will. In some cases, holographic (handwritten) wills have actually been voided by notarization because the document was not entirely in the testator's handwriting.

Exception. Advance directives for health care, popularly called "living wills," may be notarized. These are not actual wills, but written statements of the signer's wishes concerning medical treatment in the event that he or she is unable to give instructions on his or her own behalf.

Immigration Documents

Notarizing Immigration Documents. Certain immigration documents may be notarized. Non-USCIS documents are often notarized and submitted in support of an immigration or naturalization petition. These include translator's declarations, statements from employers or banks and affidavits of relationship.

Do Not Give Advice. Nonattorney Notaries may never advise others on the subject of immigration or help others to prepare immigration documents — and especially not for a fee (57 Pa. C.S. 325[a][2]). Notaries who offer immigration advice to others may be prosecuted for the unauthorized practice of law.

Authentication

Documents Sent Out of State. Documents notarized in Pennsylvania and sent out of state may be required to bear proof that the Notary's signature and seal are genuine and that the Notary had authority to act at the time of notarization. This

REVIEWING THE DOCUMENT

process of proving the genuineness of an official signature and seal is called *authentication* or *legalization*.

In Pennsylvania, the proof is in the form of an authenticating certificate attached to the notarized document by the prothonotary (clerk of the court of common pleas) in whose office the Notary filed his or her official signature or the Secretary of the Commonwealth's Certification Division. The prothonotary maintains a "Notary Register" containing signatures of Notaries within the county.

Authenticating certificates are also known as certificates of official character, certificates of authority, certificates of capacity, certificates of authenticity, certificates of prothonotary and "flags".

The fee for an authenticating certificate from a prothonotary may vary from county to county. An authenticating certificate from the Department of State, including an *apostille*, costs $15 per document (check or money order, payable to "Commonwealth of Pennsylvania").

The original notarized document, a cover letter indicating the destination state or country and an addressed, postage-paid return envelope must be sent to:

> Pennsylvania Department of State
> Bureau of Commissions,
> Elections and Legislation
> Room 210 North Office Building
> Harrisburg, PA 17120
> (717) 787-5280

It is not the Notary's responsibility to pick up or pay for the certificate of authority.

Documents Sent Out of Country. If the notarized document is going out of the United States, a chain authentication process may be necessary, and additional certificates of authority may have to be obtained from the U.S. Department of State in Washington, D.C., a foreign consulate in Washington, D.C. and a ministry of foreign affairs in the particular foreign nation.

Apostilles and The Hague Convention. Fortunately, more than 100 nations, including the United States, subscribe to a treaty under the auspices of The Hague Conference on Private International Law. The official name of this treaty, adopted by the Conference on October 5, 1961, is *The Hague*

Convention Abolishing the Requirement of Legalization for Foreign Public Documents, hereafter simply called The Hague Convention. The Hague Convention simplifies authentication of notarized documents exchanged between any of the subscribing nations. (For a list of the subscribing countries, visit *Hcch.net/index_en.php*.)

The Hague Convention. Under The Hague Convention, only one authenticating certificate called an *apostille* is necessary to ensure acceptance of a Notary's signature in these subscribing countries. (*Apostille* is French for "notation.")

In Pennsylvania, *apostilles* are issued by the Department of State. (A county prothonotary does not issue *apostilles*.) The procedure and fees are the same as for obtaining an ordinary authenticating certificate. Ensure that the country for which the document is destined is specified in the request.

Documents from Other States and Nations. If a document is lawfully notarized in another state or jurisdiction of the United States by a Notary, by a judge, clerk or deputy clerk of a court or by any other authorized official, no authentication is required. The notarization has the same effect as one performed by a Pennsylvania Notary. Pennsylvania regards the signature and title of the person performing a notarial act in another U.S. jurisdiction as evidence that the signature is genuine, that the person holds the title given and that the office gives that person the authority to notarize (57 Pa. C.S. 311[a][1-3]).

Likewise, if a document is lawfully notarized anywhere in the world by anyone acting under U.S. federal authority — including judges, clerks and deputy clerks of a court and officers of the U.S. military, foreign service or a consulate — no further authentication beyond the official's signature and title is required by Pennsylvania (57 Pa. C.S. 313[a][1-4]).

If a document is lawfully notarized in a foreign nation by a foreign Notary, by a judge, clerk or deputy clerk of a court of that nation, a person authorized to perform notarial acts by law of a federally recognized Indian tribe or nation or by any other official authorized by that nation's laws to perform notarial acts, no authentication is required (57 Pa. C.S. 312, 314[1-2]). ■

Common Notary Acts

Authorized Acts

Pennsylvania Notaries may perform the following notarial acts (57 Pa. C.S. 305[a-e]):

- Acknowledgments. Certifying that a signer personally appeared before the Notary, was identified by the Notary and acknowledged signing the document (See pages 24–26).

- Oaths and Affirmations. Certifying that an individual personally appeared before the Notary, was identified by the Notary and took an oath or affirmation either verbally or in writing (See pages 26–27).

- Verifications upon Oath or Affirmation (Jurats). Certifying that a signer personally appeared before the Notary, was identified by the Notary, swore or affirmed in the Notary's presence that the statements in the document are true and then signed the document in the Notary's presence (See pages 31–29).

- Witnessing or Attestation of Signatures. Certifying that a signer personally appeared before the Notary, was identified by the Notary, and signed the document in the Notary's presence (See page 29).

- Copy Certifications. Certifying that a photocopy of an original document, presented to the Notary, is a true and complete copy (See page 30).

Acknowledgments

Purpose. Acknowledgments are the most common form of notarization. The main purpose of the acknowledgment is positive identification of the document signer and verification that the signer freely signed the document for the purposes stated therein.

In executing an acknowledgment and completing the acknowledgment certificate, the Notary certifies three things (57 Pa. C.S. 305[a][1-2]):

1) The signer *personally appeared* before the Notary on the date and in the county indicated on the Notary certificate. (A notarization cannot be based upon a telephone call or on a Notary's familiarity with a signature.)

2) The signer was *positively identified* by the Notary through personal knowledge or other satisfactory evidence (See "Identifying Document Signers" pages 11–13), and the Notary compared the signature on the document to the identification presented.

3) The signer *acknowledged* to the Notary that the signature was freely made for the purposes stated in the document and, if the document was signed in a representative capacity, that he or she had proper authority to do so. If a document is willingly signed in the presence of the Notary, this act serves as an acknowledgment.

Witnessing Signature Not Required. For an acknowledgment, the document does not have to be signed in the Notary's presence. Rather, the document signer needs to acknowledge that he or she made the signature. As long as the signer appears before the Notary with the signed document at the time of notarization to acknowledge having signed it, the Notary may execute the acknowledgment.

Who May Take Acknowledgments. Within the Commonwealth, Notaries and the following officials may take acknowledgments in their jurisdictions (57 Pa. C.S. 310[a][3]):

1) A judge of a court of record.

2) A clerk, deputy clerk, prothonotary or deputy prothonotary of a court having a seal.

3) A recorder of deeds, deputy recorder of deeds, justice of the peace, magistrate or alderman.

Certificates for Acknowledgment

Pennsylvania law provides the following short form acknowledgment certificate that accommodates signers in an individual capacity. Notaries must use wording substantially similar to the following (57 Pa.C.S.A. 316[1]). To see the list of certificates available to Notaries when notarizing for signers acting in representative capacities, visit *Nationalnotary.org/pennsylvania/supplies/notarycertificates*.

- Individual Acknowledgment Certificate — for an individual or individuals signing in an individual capacity:

State of Pennsylvania
County of _____

This record was acknowledged before me on _____ (date) by _____(name(s) of individual(s))

_____

Signature of notarial officer   (Stamp of Notary)
Title of office _____
My commission expires: _____

Acknowledgment by Attorney at Law

<u>Purpose</u>. In executing an Acknowledgment by Attorney at Law (referred to in other jurisdictions as a "Proof of Execution by Subscribing Witness"), a Notary certifies that the signature of a person who does not appear before the Notary (the principal signer) is genuine and freely made based on the sworn testimony of a member of the Pennsylvania Bar who does appear as a subscribing (signing) witness.

An Acknowledgment by Attorney at Law is used when the principal signer is out of town or otherwise unavailable to appear before a Notary. This act should never be used merely because the principal signer prefers not to take the time to personally appear before a Notary. Because of the high potential for fraud, an Acknowledgment by Attorney at Law should be used only when there is no other option.

Only by an Attorney. In Pennsylvania, only an attorney who is a member of the Pennsylvania Bar may act as a subscribing witness for an acknowledging principal (57 Pa. C.S. 316[2.1]).

Verifying Bar Status. The Notary must be satisfied that the attorney making the acknowledgment is a member of the Pennsylvania Bar. The certificate prescribed by Pennsylvania law states that the Notary personally knows or has satisfactory proof that the witnessing attorney is "a member of the bar of the highest court of [the] state." Documentary evidence such as a Pennsylvania Bar membership card may suffice (57 Pa. C.S. 316[2.1]).

Oath (Affirmation) for the Attorney. In other jurisdictions, oaths are customarily administered to subscribing witnesses to compel truthfulness. However, Pennsylvania law does not require an attorney at law serving as a subscribing witness to take such an oath. It is recommended, however, that the attorney sign the Notary's journal.

Oaths and Affirmations

Definition of Terms. An oath is a solemn, spoken pledge to a Supreme Being. An affirmation is a solemn, spoken pledge on one's own personal honor, with no reference to a Supreme Being. A person who objects to taking an oath — pledging to a Supreme Being — may instead make an affirmation, which does not refer to a Supreme Being. Both are usually a promise of truthfulness and have the same legal effect.

Purpose. The primary purpose of oaths and affirmations is to compel truthfulness in the person taking the oath or affirmation both by appealing to his or her conscience and by arousing his or her fear of legal repercussions. In taking an oath or making an affirmation in an official proceeding, a person may be subject to criminal penalties for perjury should he or she fail to be truthful or to follow through on the pledge or promise made.

An oath or affirmation can be a full-fledged notarial act in its own right, as when giving an oath of office to a public official, or it can be part of another notarial act, as when executing a jurat or swearing in a credible identifying witness.

When administering an oath or affirmation as a stand-alone notarial act, the Notary is not typically asked to complete a Notary certificate.

COMMON NOTARY ACTS

<u>Ceremony and Gestures</u>. To reinforce upon the person taking the oath or affirmation the importance of truthfulness, the Notary is encouraged to lend a sense of ceremony and formality to the oath or affirmation. During administration of an oath or affirmation, the Notary and the person taking the oath or affirmation traditionally raise their right hands, though this is not a legal requirement.

When administering an oath or affirmation, the individual taking the oath must swear or affirm that the statements contained in the oath are true or that the individual will perform an act or duty faithfully and truthfully. The oath may be either verbal or in writing.

<u>Wording for Oath (or Affirmation)</u>. If law or rule does not prescribe otherwise, a Pennsylvania Notary may use the following or similar words in administering an oath (or affirmation):

- Oath (affirmation) for an affiant signing an affidavit or a deponent signing a deposition:

   Do you solemnly swear that the statements in this document are true to the best of your knowledge and belief, so help you God?

   (Do you solemnly affirm that the statements in this document are true to the best of your knowledge and belief?)

- Oath (affirmation) for a credible identifying witness identifying a document signer who is in the Notary's presence:

   Do you solemnly swear that you personally know this signer truly holds the identity he (or she) claims, so help you God?

   (Do you solemnly affirm that you personally know this signer truly holds the identity he [or she] claims?)

Verifications upon Oath or Affirmation

<u>Purpose</u>. The purpose of this act is to certify that the signer swore to or affirmed the truthfulness of statements in a document that he or she signed in the Notary's presence. Because a jurat requires an oath or affirmation, this notarial act compels truthfulness by appealing to the signer's conscience and fear of criminal penalties for perjury.

Requirements. In executing a jurat and completing the jurat certificate, a Notary certifies four things (57 Pa. C.S. 305 [b][1] & [2]):

1) The signer *personally appeared* before the Notary on the date and in the county indicated on the Notary certificate. (A notarization cannot be based upon a telephone call or on a Notary's familiarity with a signature.)

2) The signer was *positively identified* by the Notary through personal knowledge or other satisfactory evidence.

3) The Notary *administered an oath or affirmation* to the signer, who swore or affirmed that the statements in the document are true.

4) The Notary *watched the signer* sign the document at the time of notarization and compared the signature to the identification presented.

Acknowledgment vs. Jurat. The main differences between acknowledgments and jurats — the two most common forms of notarization — are the following:

- The acknowledgment requires the principal to acknowledge that the signature on the document is his or her own, that it was made willingly and, if the document was signed in a representative capacity, that he or she had proper authority to do so.

- A jurat requires the principal to sign the document in the Notary's presence. The jurat requires the principal to take an oath from or make an affirmation to the Notary regarding the contents of the document; the acknowledgment does not.

Certificate for Verification

The following jurat certificate wording is sufficient per Pennsylvania statute (57 Pa. C.S. 316[3]):

State of Pennsylvania

County of _____

Signed and sworn to (or affirmed) before me on _____ (date) by _____ (names[s] of individual[s] making statement).

_____
(Signature of Notary)   (Stamp of Notary)

Title of office _____

My commission expires: _____

Affidavits and Depositions

<u>Affidavits vs. Depositions</u>. Both of these terms refer to a document containing a statement voluntarily signed and sworn to or affirmed before a Notary or other official with oath administering powers. The signer of an affidavit is called the affiant; the signer of a deposition is called the deponent. Either type of document may require a jurat.

<u>Purpose of an Affidavit</u>. Affidavits are used in and out of court for a wide variety of purposes, from declaring losses to an insurance company to attesting to the accuracy of a translation. An affidavit is the sworn statement of an individual.

<u>Purpose of a Deposition</u>. A deposition is a transcript of the deponent's oral statements, so it begins as a verbal process and ends as a written one. Depositions are used only in lawsuits or other judicial proceedings. A deposition permits the opposing party in the lawsuit to cross-examine the deponent, with the questions and responses included in the deposition's text.

Witnessing or Attestation of a Signature

<u>Purpose</u>. The purpose of this act is to certify that the signer signed the document in the Notary's presence.

<u>Requirements</u>. In witnessing a signature and completing the certificate, a Notary certifies three things (4 Pa. Code 167.63[a-d]):

1) The signer *personally appeared* before the Notary on the date and in the county indicated on the Notary certificate.

2) The signer was *positively identified* by the Notary through personal knowledge or other satisfactory evidence.

3) The Notary *watched the signer sign* the document at the time of notarization and compared the signature to the identification presented.

Certificate for Witnessing or Attesting a Signature

The following signature witnessing certificate wording is sufficient per Pennsylvania statute (57 Pa. C.S. 316[4]):

State of Pennsylvania

County of _____

Signed (or attested) before me on _____ (date) by _____ (names[s] of individual[s] making statement).

_____
(Signature of Notary)   (Stamp of Notary)

Title of office _____

My commission expires: _____

Copy Certifications

<u>Definition</u>. When a Notary certifies a copy of a document, he or she is certifying only that it is a complete and accurate transcription or reproduction of the record or item (57 Pa. C.S. 305 [d]). Before completing the Notary certificate, the Notary should compare the photocopy to the original to be sure that the copy is indeed complete and correct: that the copy is legible, that no text has been cut off, etc.

The certification does not mean the Notary attests to the accuracy or validity of the contents of the document.

A Notarial Officer who certifies or attests a copy of a record or an item which was copied shall determine that the copy is a complete and accurate transcription or reproduction of the record or item. The Notary must make sure that the copy is exactly the same as the original.

Pennsylvania Notaries may not certify certain federal, state or county records. Only the agencies where these records are filed may certify copies, because they alone hold the original documents or records. This would include the following types of documents:

- Birth records

- Death records

- Marriage records

- Corporate records, i.e. Articles of Incorporation

Certificate for Copy Certification

Pennsylvania statute says the following Notary certificate is sufficient for certifying a copy of a document (57 Pa. C.S. 316[5]):

State of Pennsylvania

County of _____

I certify that this is a true and correct copy of a _____ (document type) in the possession of _____ (name of person who presents the document).

Dated _____

_____
(Signature of Notary)   (Stamp of Notary)

Title of Office: _____

My commission expires: _____

Certified Copies of Notarial Records

<u>Procedure</u>. Members of the public may request Notary certified photocopies of entries in the Notary's official journal or of any notarial record in the Notary's office (57 Pa. C.S. 319[g.1]).

<u>Inspection and Certified Copies of Notary Journals</u>. A notary public must permit inspection of the journal to any person requesting to view the journal. A notary public can prove that a notarial act took place by supplying a certified copy of the journal entry. To make a certified copy of an entry in the journal, the notary public reproduces the page and attaches a certificate stating, "I certify that this is a true and correct copy from my official journal in my possession." The reproduction should be a photocopy of the entire register page containing the entry in question. A notary must give a certified copy of the journal to a person that applies for it. Requests may, but are not required to be, in writing. The notary public shall provide the certified copy

within 10 days of receipt of the request. The notary may charge reasonable fees for copying and postage, but the requestor should be advised in advance of these fees. If the scope of the request is not clear, the notary may offer to have the requester inspect the journal at the notary's office to identify the specific pages or dates that the requester is seeking. A request for inspection or certified copies of a notary journal made through an investigative request by law enforcement or by the Department or in a subpoena in the course of criminal or civil litigation must be complied with in the manner specified in the request or subpoena.

Motor Vehicle Title Duties

Motor Vehicle Attestations. Pennsylvania Notaries may serve as "card agents" in processing paperwork related to the title and transfer of motor vehicles. The Pennsylvania Department of Transportation requires that certain statements concerning drivers and their vehicles be made under oath. A discussion of the Notary's role in this specialized area is beyond the scope of this book. For further information, please contact the Pennsylvania Department of Transportation, Driver and Vehicle Services at (800) 932-4600 or (717) 391-6190.

Protests

Definition. A protest is a written statement by a Notary or other authorized officer that a payment has not been received. The protest must (57 Pa. C.S. 305[e]):

- Identify the negotiable instrument.

- Certify either the presentment has been made or, if not made, the reason why.

- State that the instrument has been dishonored by non-acceptance or nonpayment.

- The protest may also certify that the notice of dishonor has been given to some or all parties.

Purpose. In rare instances, Pennsylvania Notaries may be asked to protest the nonpayment of a negotiable instrument, such as a bank draft or bill of exchange.

COMMON NOTARY ACTS

Requirements. The individual requesting the protest must appear before the Notary, be identified by either personal knowledge or satisfactory evidence, and be identified in the protest as the holder of the dishonored negotiable instrument (4 Pa. Code 167.66[c-d]).

Special Knowledge Required. Notarial acts of protest are complicated and varied, requiring a special knowledge of financial and legal terminology. Unless a Notary is employed by a depository institution and the protest is made or noted within the scope of employment, the Notary may not make or note a protest of a negotiable instrument.

Notary Services Fees

Maximum Fees. The maximum fee for executing a notarial act is set by the Secretary of the Commonwealth. A Notary may charge these fees, a lesser fee or not charge at all. A Notary who willfully overcharges may have his or her commission revoked. The maximum fees that a Notary Public may charge for Notary services are as follows (4 Pa. Code 161.2):

- Acknowledgments — $5. For taking an acknowledgment, the Notary may charge $5 for the first signature on a document, plus $2 for each additional signature on that same document.

- Taking verification on oath or affirmation — $5 no matter how many signatures.

- Certifying or attesting a copy or deposition — $5 per copy certified.

- Witness or attestation of a signature — $5 for each signature witnessed.

- Oaths and affirmations — $5 for administering an oath or affirmation with or without certificate and seal, $5 per individual.

- Protests — $3 for protesting a bill or note, the fee is $3 per page.

- All other notarial acts — $5 for performing any lawful notarial act other than listed above, $5.

- Travel and clerical fees. A Notary may charge a clerical or administrative fee for services related to a notarial act, such as copying, postage, travel and telephone calls. If charging clerical or administrative fees, the Notary must inform the customer of the amount of each fee prior to performing the service. Fees must be reasonable (4 Pa. Code 161.2[d]).

- Overcharging. A notary public may not charge or receive a notary public fee in excess of the fee fixed by the department (57 Pa. C.S. 329.1[b]).

Receipt for Fees. A Notary must provide an itemized receipt for all fees charged.

Employer and Notary Agreement. The fee for a Notary public:

1) shall be the property of the Notary; and

2) unless mutually agreed by the Notary and the employer, must not belong to or be received by the entity that employs the Notary (57 Pa. C.S. 329.1[d]).

Posting of Fees Required. The Notary fees must be posted in a prominent location in the Notary's place of business or provided on request to anyone using the Notary's services. However, if a Notary does not charge a fee, the requirement to display or provide fees does not apply (57 Pa. C.S. 329.1[c]).

Option Not to Charge. Notaries are not required to charge for their Notary services, and they may charge any fee less than the statutory maximum. A Notary who does not charge for performing notarial acts is not required to post a table of fees (57 Pa. C.S. 3329.1[c][2]). ■

Notary Journal

Journal of Notarial Acts

<u>Requirement</u>. Pennsylvania Notaries are required to make an accurate chronological record of every notarial act in a journal. The journal can be created either on a tangible medium (i.e., on paper), or in an electronic format. Pennsylvania Notaries can keep a separate journal for tangible records and electronic records. If the journal is maintained on a tangible medium, it must be bound with numbered pages. Electronic journals must be in a tamper-evident electronic format complying with the regulations of the Department (57 Pa. C.S. 319[b]).

<u>Required Journal Entries</u>. An entry in a journal shall be made contemporaneously with performance of the notarial act and contain all of the following information (57 Pa. C.S. 319[c]):

1) The date and time of the notarial act.

2) A description of the document, if any, and type of notarial act.

3) The full name and address (city and state) of each individual for whom the notarial act is performed.

4) The method used to identify the signer. If the identity is based on personal knowledge, a statement to that effect. If satisfactory evidence is used to identify the signer, a brief description of the method of identification and any identification credential presented, including the date of issuance and expiration (57 Pa.C.S.). If a credible identifying witness is used, they should sign the journal in

the identification section. The Notary should also make a notation in the journal that a credible witness was used for identification.

5) The fee charged by the Notary. If a fee is waived, the Notary must indicate this in the journal using "n/c" or "0" (zero) or a similar notation. Clerical and administrative fees must be separately itemized in the journal (Department of State website "Fees").

Optional Entries. In addition to the required journal entries, a Notary journal may contain the signature of the individual for whom the notarial act is performed and any additional information about a specific transaction which might assist the Notary to recall the transaction. For example, Notaries may enter the address and telephone number of every witness, as well as the address where the notarization was performed, if it was somewhere other than the Notary's office. When a signer is acting in a representative capacity — as an attorney in fact, trustee, guardian, corporate officer or the like — the Notary should include the signer's capacity in the journal. Finally, in some cases a description of the document signer's demeanor ("The signer appeared very nervous") or notations about the identity of other persons who were present may also be pertinent.

Prohibited Entries. A journal may not contain any personal financial or identification information, such as complete Social Security numbers, complete drivers' license numbers or complete account numbers.

Recording Document Dates

If the document has a specific date on it, the Notary should record that date in the journal of notarial acts. Often the only date on a document is the date of the signature that is being notarized. If the signature is undated, however, the document may have no date on it at all. In that case, the Notary should record "no date" or "undated" in the journal.

Acknowledgment and Jurat Date Requirements. For acknowledgments, the date the document was signed must either precede or be the same as the date of the notarization; it may not follow it. For a jurat, the date the document was signed and the date of the notarization must be the same.

A document whose signature is dated after the date on its Notary certificate risks rejection by a recorder, who may question how the document could have been notarized before it was signed.

Journal Thumbprint

Many Notaries are asking document signers to leave a thumbprint in the journal. The journal thumbprint protects the Notary against claims that a signer did not appear and is a strong deterrent to forgery, because it represents absolute proof of the signer's identity and appearance before the Notary.

Provided the signer is willing, nothing prevents a Notary from asking for a thumbprint for every notarial act. Since a thumbprint is not required by law, however, the Notary may not refuse to notarize if the signer declines to leave one.

Complete Entry Before Certificate

Good Practice. The prudent Notary completes the journal entry before filling out the Notary certificate on a document. This prevents the signer from leaving with the notarized document before vital information can be entered in the journal.

Inspection and Copying

Inspection of Notary Records. Since the Notary's official journal is kept for the public benefit, members of the public may lawfully ask to examine it (Department of State website "Notary Public Equipment").

Notaries Must Protect Signers' Personal Information. Because the journal must be kept in the Notary's place of business, this means that it must be open to public inspection during the Notary's normal business hours. Although others are allowed to inspect the journal, the Notary should never be relaxed about its security. Notaries must protect the privacy and personal information of signers by not allowing random or unsupervised examination of the journal. Anyone wishing to inspect the journal should indicate the approximate date and nature of the transaction and the signer's name, so the Notary can locate the specific entry sought.

Pennsylvania Notaries should "maintain custody and control" of the journal. In addition, the prudent Notary will request identification from anyone who wants to inspect the journal. The

Notary may, in fact, treat a journal inspection in the same fashion as a notarization, asking the individual to sign the journal and recording the person's address and ID information.

Certified Copy of Journal Entry. A Notary must give a certified copy of the journal to a person that applies for it (57 Pa. C.S. 319[g.1]).

Journal Ownership

Surrender of Journal. A Notary's journal is the exclusive property of the Notary and may not be surrendered to an employer upon termination of employment (57 Pa.C.S. 319[e]).

Journal Loss or Theft

If a stamping device or journal is lost or stolen, the Notary must notify the Department within 15 days of discovering the loss or theft. The term "loss" includes equipment that is misplaced, destroyed or otherwise made unavailable. The notification must include a statement that the Notary does not possess the stamping device and/or journal and the date the Notary discovered that the stamping device and/or journal was lost or stolen. A Notary may wish to file a police report for stolen items (57 Pa. C.S. 319[d]).

Disposition of Journal

Termination of Office. A Notary must deliver the journal to the office of the Recorder of Deeds in the county where the Notary last maintained an office within 30 days when the Notary's commission expires (and is not renewed), the Notary resigns, or if the Notary's commission is revoked (57 Pa.C.S. 319[e]).

Death or Incompetency. On the death or adjudication of incompetency of a current or former Notary, the personal representative, guardian, or a person knowingly in the possession of the journal shall deliver it within 30 days to the office of the Recorder of Deeds in the county where the Notary last maintained an office (57 Pa.C.S. 319[g]). ■

Notary Certificate

Certificate Requirement and Purpose

Requirement. In notarizing any document, a Notary must complete a Notary certificate. When filling in the blanks in the Notary certificate, Notaries should either type or print neatly in dark ink. This certificate must be completed contemporaneously with the performance of the notarial act (57 Pa. C.S. 315 [a][2][i]).

Purpose. The certificate is wording that indicates exactly what the Notary has certified. The Notary certificate may be typed or printed on the document itself or on an attachment to it.

By completing and signing a Notary certificate, the Notary certifies that he or she has complied with the requirements and made the determinations specified by law for that particular notarization (57 Pa. C.S. 315[d]). The certificate does not indicate that the Notary knows the accuracy or validity of the contents of the attached document.

Parts of the Certificate

Required Components. In Pennsylvania, the certificate must contain the following (57 Pa. C.S. 315[a], 316):

1) The *venue* indicates where the notarization is being performed. Pennsylvania statute requires venue wording to be substantially as follows: "State of Pennsylvania, County of ____," with the county of notarization inserted in the blank. "Commonwealth of Pennsylvania" may be used in lieu of "State of Pennsylvania" on certificates.

2) The *statement of particulars* indicates what the notarization

has certified. Under Pennsylvania law, the statement of particulars must include the name of the person whose signature is being notarized. When the notarial act does not involve a signature — for example, a copy certification or the administration of an oath of office — the certificate must include the name of the person requesting the notarial act.

3) The *official signature of the Notary* must be signed exactly as it appears on the commission, or executed electronically in a manner which attributes the signature to the Notary Public identified in the commission. The Notary also must include the date on which he or she signed. If the Notary's signature is illegible, the Notary must print his or her name legibly next to the Notary signature.

4) The title Notary Public and the commission expiration date.

5) The *official stamp of the Notary* should be placed near the Notary's signature in a form capable of photographic reproduction. If an electronic record is used, an official stamp may be attached to or logically associated with the certificate.

Completing or Correcting the Certificate

Correcting the Certificate. When filling out the certificate, the Notary needs to make sure any preprinted information is accurate. For example, the venue — the state and county in which the notarial act is taking place — may have been filled in prior to the notarization. If the preprinted venue is incorrect, the Notary must line through the incorrect state and/or county, write in the proper site of the notarization, and initial and date the change.

Attached Certificate Forms

Attaching Certificates. When certificate wording is not preprinted on the document, a certificate form on a separate sheet may be attached by the Notary. This form is typically stapled to the document's left margin following the signature page.

If the attached certificate form is replacing unacceptable preprinted wording, the Notary should line through the preprinted wording and write below, "See attached certificate." If the document has no preprinted wording, however, the Notary should not add this notation. Those words could be viewed as an unauthorized change to the document.

To prevent an attached certificate from being removed and fraudulently placed on another document, the Notary may write a brief description of the document on the certificate: "This certificate is attached to a (title or type of document), dated _____, of (number) pages, signed by (name[s] of signer[s])."

<u>Notary's Responsibility</u>. While fraud-deterrent steps such as the above can make it much more difficult for attached certificate forms to be removed and misused, there is no absolute protection against removal and misuse.

However, while the certificate remains in the Notary's control, it is the Notary's responsibility to ensure that the certificate is securely attached only to its intended document. In this instance, 'securely attached' means stapled or otherwise bound; it does not include tape, paper clips or binder clips (57 Pa. C.S. 315[f]).

Do Not Pre-Sign or Pre-Seal Certificates

<u>Avoid Potential Fraud</u>. Pennsylvania law prohibits a Notary from signing a certificate until the notarial act has been completed (57 Pa. C.S. 315[e]).

A Notary must never give or mail an unattached, signed and stamped certificate form to another person and trust that person to attach it to a particular document, even if asked to do so by a signer who previously appeared before the Notary.

These actions could facilitate fraud or forgery and, since such actions would be indefensible in a civil court of law, they could subject the Notary to lawsuits to recover damages resulting from the Notary's negligence or misconduct.

Selecting Certificates

<u>Unauthorized Practice of Law</u>. Nonattorney Notaries should never select Notary certificates for any transaction. It is not the role of a nonattorney Notary to decide what type of certificate — and thus what type of notarization — a document needs. As ministerial officials, Notaries generally follow instructions and complete forms that have been provided for them; they do not issue instructions or decide which forms are appropriate in a given case. If a document is presented to a Notary without certificate wording and if the signer does not know what type of notarial act is appropriate, the signer should be asked to find

out what kind of notarization and certificate are needed. Usually the agency that issued or will be accepting the document can provide this information. A Notary who selects certificates may be engaging in the unauthorized practice of law. ■

Notary Stamp

Requirement
A Pennsylvania Notary is required to use an official stamp to authenticate all acts, instruments and attestations (57 Pa. C.S. 317[1]).

Obtaining an Official Stamp
Upon receipt of his or her initial Certificate of Appointment, the Notary must obtain an official stamp. To do so, the Notary must present to any stamp or seal vendor or manufacturer, in person or by mail, the original or a certified copy of the Certificate of Appointment.

It is illegal for a person or agency to make, manufacture, or otherwise produce a Pennsylvania Notary stamp without the necessary Certificate of Appointment. This statute applies to both original and replacement stamps.

Stamp Format and Type
Rubber Stamp. The official seal must be a rubber stamp and must be photographically reproducible (57 Pa. C.S. 317[1-3]).

Ink Color. The National Notary Association recommends that Notaries use either black or very dark-colored ink, since this is the preference of county recorders, who find that dark ink microfilms easily.

Stamp Format. The Pennsylvania Notary stamp must have a maximum height of one inch and width of three and one-half inches, with a plain border (57 Pa. C.S. 317[2]).

Required Information. Within the plain border, the components of the seal must appear in the following order (57 Pa.C.S.317[1]):

1) "Commonwealth of Pennsylvania" – "Notary Seal";

2) Name of Notary as it appears on the commission and the words "Notary Public";

3) Name of county in which the Notary maintains an office;

4) Commission expiration date;

5) Seven-digit identification number assigned by the Department of State.

Embossing Seal

An embosser may be used during a notarial act, but only in conjunction with the use of an official Notary stamp (57 Pa. C.S. 317[3]).

Stamp Placement

The Notary's official stamp impression should be placed on the Notary certificate and as close to the signature as is reasonably possible. Pennsylvania Notaries may not, however, affix their stamp over any signature on the document or any text on the certificate (57 Pa. C.S. 315 [b][1]).

No Room for Stamp. Some public recorders will reject documents if writing or document text intrudes within the borders of the Notary's stamp or seal.

If there is not enough room on a document for the Notary's stamp and signature, then the Notary may have no choice but to complete and attach a certificate form that duplicates the Notary wording on the document.

Smeared or Illegible Stamp

Do Not Attempt to Fix a Seal Impression. If an initial stamp impression is unreadable and there is ample room on the document, another impression can be affixed nearby. The illegibility of the first impression will indicate why a second stamp impression was necessary. The Notary should then record in the journal that a second impression was applied.

A Notary should never attempt to fix an imperfect stamp impression with pen, ink or correction fluid. This may be viewed as evidence of tampering and cause the document to be rejected by a receiving agency.

Seal Ownership and Security

A Notary must keep the seal in a secure location — either in the sole possession of the Notary or in a locked location over which the Notary has sole control — during any period in which the Notary Public is not using the stamp to perform a notarial act (57 Pa. C.S. 318[a][1]).

Pennsylvania law specifically prohibits a Notary from allowing or authorizing any other person to use his or her official stamp (57 Pa. C.S. 318[a][1]).

Surrender of Stamp

If a Notary's commission is suspended or revoked, the Notary must deliver the seal of office to the Department of State within 10 days after the notice of suspension or revocation (57 Pa. C.S. 318[a][2.1]).

Disposition and Disposal of Stamp

If a Notary resigns or the expiration date on the stamp expires, the Notary must disable the stamping device by destroying, defacing, damaging, erasing or securing it against use in a manner which renders it unusable (57 Pa. C.S. 318.2).

Upon the death or adjudication of incompetency of a Notary, the personal representative or guardian or any person knowingly in possession of the stamp, shall destroy it by rendering it unusable (57 Pa. C.S. 318.3).

An individual whose notary public commission has been suspended or revoked shall surrender possession of the stamping device to the department (57 Pa. C.S. 318[a][2.1]).

Seal Loss or Theft

<u>Replacing the Stamp</u>. If a stamping device or journal is lost or stolen, the Notary shall notify the Department within 15 days of discovering the loss or theft. The term "loss" includes equipment that is misplaced, destroyed or otherwise made unavailable. The notification must include a statement that the Notary does not possess the stamping device and/or journal and the date the Notary discovered that the stamping device and/or journal was lost or stolen. A Notary may wish to file a police report for stolen items (57 Pa. C.S. 318[b]). ∎

Electronic Notarization

E-Notarization Rules and Procedures

eNotarizations are Regulated by the State. A Notary Public who wishes to perform notarial acts with respect to electronic records must be authorized by the Department to act as an "electronic Notary" or "e-Notary" prior to performing any acts with respect to electronic records. To obtain authorization, a Notary must submit the following information to the Department in a manner prescribed by the Department:

- Name of Notary Public

- Commission number

- Office address

- Email address

- Name of electronic notarization solution provider

- Contact information for solution provider

- Website for solution provider

Tamper-Evident Technology. A notary public may select one or more tamper-evident technologies to perform notarial acts with respect to electronic records. A person may not require a notary public to perform a notarial act with respect to an electronic record with a technology that the notary public has not selected (57 Pa.C.S. 320[a]).

ELECTRONIC NOTARIZATION

Technology Neutrality. [T]he department may promulgate regulations to implement this chapter.

Regulations regarding the performance of notarial acts with respect to electronic records may not require or accord greater legal status or effect to the implementation or application of a specific technology or technical specification (57 Pa.C.S. 327[a]).

Notification and Registration.

1) Before a notary public performs the initial notarial act with respect to an electronic record, a notary public shall notify the department that the notary public will be performing notarial acts with respect to electronic records and identify each technology the notary public intends to use.

2) If the department has established standards for approval of technology under section 327 (relating to regulations), the technology must conform to the standards. If the technology conforms to the standards, the department shall approve the use of the technology" (57 Pa.C.S. 320[b]).

All requirements of a notarial act performed with respect to a paper (hard copy) record also apply to an electronic record. These requirements include: personal appearance and identification of the signer, completion of the Notary certificate, use of an official Notary stamp and recording of the act in the Notary journal.

Educational Requirement. The three hours of Notary education required for all applicants must include an introduction to electronic notarization and an overview of the current status of electronic notarizations within the Commonwealth.

Electronic Seals

Electronic Notarization. The "Electronic Transactions Act" of 1999 permits a Notary to notarize an electronic document or signature without the use of a seal, if the following information is attached to or logically associated with the electronic record being notarized (73 P.S. 2260.307):

1) The Notary's full name and the words "Notary Public."

2) The name of the Notary's county and municipality.

3) The Notary's commission expiration date.

Electronic Signatures

Uniform Real Property Electronic Recording Act (URPERA). Effective July 5, 2012, Pennsylvania enacted the URPERA, which authorizes county Recorders of Deeds to receive electronic real property deeds, mortgages, releases and other documents affecting title to real property for recordation. The URPERA also permits a Notary to use an electronic signature in notarizing an electronic real property document without affixing an image of the Notary's official physical seal.

Attribution of Notary's E-signature. A Notary must execute his or her electronic signature in a manner that attributes the signature to the Notary identified on the commission (57 Pa.C.S.A. 315 [a][3][1][B]).

Electronic Journal

Form and Content of an Electronic Journal. A journal of a Notary Public maintained in electronic format may be in any form that meets the journal and entry requirements of paper journals.

(a) A journal of a Notary Public maintained in electronic format shall be designed to prevent the insertion, removal or substitution of an entry.

(b) A journal of a Notary Public maintained in electronic format shall be securely stored and recoverable in the event of a hardware or software malfunction.

(c) Entries from the notarial journal must be available upon demand by the Department in a PDF format.

(d) If a signature of a signer is contained in an electronic Notary journal, the signature must be:

1) Attached to or logically associated with the electronic journal.

2) Linked to the data in such a manner that any subsequent

ELECTRONIC NOTARIZATION

alterations to the electronic Notary journal entry are detectable and may invalidate the electronic notarial journal entry.

(e) A journal of a Notary Public maintained in electronic format which is delivered to the office of the Recorder of Deeds must be delivered in a format prescribed by the receiving Recorder of Deeds (57 Pa. C.S. 319[e]). ∎

Prohibited Actions & Administrative Penalties

Prohibited Acts

Unauthorized Practice of Law. A Notary may not give legal advice or accept fees for legal advice. As a ministerial officer, the nonattorney Notary is generally not permitted to assist other persons in drafting, preparing, selecting, completing or understanding a document or transaction.

Failure to Affix Seal Impression. A Notary must not fail to attach a seal impression to any document he or she notarizes. An instrument missing the official seal may be considered invalid. A Notary may be subject to civil action by aggrieved parties.

Withholding Records. Except as otherwise allowed by law, a Notary may not withhold access to or possession of an original record provided by a person that seeks performance of a notarial act by the Notary Public (57 Pa.C.S. 325[e]).

Marriages. Pennsylvania Notaries are not authorized to perform marriages unless the Notary is a member of the clergy or an official authorized to solemnize marriages.

Telephone Notarizations. Performing a notarization over the telephone is not permitted. A document signer must appear before the Notary, face-to-face in the same room, at the time of notarization.

Notarize with Direct Interest. A Notary may not notarize in any transaction in which the Notary has a direct interest, whether financial or not.

Notarize with Pecuniary Interest. A Notary may not notarize in any transaction in which the Notary has a financial interest.

Notarize Under Another Name. A Notary must sign Notary certificates in the name under which he or she was commissioned — the name that appears on the commission paper. No other name may be used.

Impersonate a Notary. The use of a Notary seal by a person other than the Notary named on the seal is considered impersonating a Notary Public, a criminal offense that could result in imprisonment for up to five years and/or a fine of up to $10,000.

Denial, Suspension or Revocation of Commission

Authority of Secretary of the Commonwealth. The Pennsylvania Secretary of the Commonwealth may, for good cause, revoke the commission of a Notary Public. Possible reasons for the denial, suspension or revocation of a Notary's commission include:

Application Misstatement or Omission. The Secretary of the Commonwealth may deny a Notary commission to any applicant who submits an application containing a material misstatement or omission of fact (57 Pa.C.S.A. 323[a][2]).

Prior Notary Commission Revoked. An applicant who has had a prior Notary commission revoked, denied, refused to renew, or suspended by any state may be denied a Notary commission (57 Pa.C.S.A. 323[a][8]).

Incompatible Offense. A finding against or admission of liability by the applicant or Notary Public in a legal proceeding or disciplinary action based on the fraud, dishonesty or deceit of the applicant or notary public may be denied a Notary commission (57 Pa.C.S.A. 323[a][4]).

Overcharging. If a Notary charges more than the legally prescribed fees, the Notary's commission may be revoked by the Secretary of the Commonwealth (57 Pa. C.S. 323.a[1]).

Failure to Require Personal Appearance. A Notary who performs a notarization when the signer, oath-taker or affirmant does not personally appear before the Notary at the time of notarization may have the commission revoked by the Secretary of the Commonwealth (57 Pa.C.S.A. 323 [a][5]).

Failure to Maintain Residency. A Notary who moves his or her residence and place of employment out of Pennsylvania vacates the office of Notary. Such a move has the same effect as resignation 57 Pa.C.S.A. 321 [d.2][2][f][1].

Disposition of Records. If removed from office, the Notary must deliver the Notary's register and public papers to the Recorder of Deeds of the county in which the Notary maintains an office within 30 days (57 Pa. C.S. 323[a][5]).

Failure to Surrender Seal. A Notary Public who resigns, or whose commission is revoked, or whose application for renewal is rejected, must deliver his or her seal of office to the Department of State within 15 days (per Secretary of State website "Notary Equipment") after resigning or receiving notice (57 Pa. C.S. 323[a][5]).

Issuing Check with Insufficient Funds. The Secretary of the Commonwealth may revoke the commission of a Notary Public who issues an insufficient funds personal check to any agency of the Commonwealth (4 Pa. Code 165.1[c][1]).

Civil Lawsuit

Liable for All Damages. A person injured by the failure, refusal or neglect of a Notary may sue to recover damages. As a ministerial official, a Pennsylvania Notary is liable for all damages caused by intentional or unintentional misconduct or neglect. The $10,000 bond offers no protection to the Notary, since the Notary will be required to reimburse the bonding firm for any funds paid out to a victim of the Notary's misconduct. An injured party may seek financial recovery for the full extent of damages in a civil lawsuit against the Notary.

Appeal of Penalty

Hearing. A Notary whose commission has been revoked by the Secretary of the Commonwealth has the right to notice, hearing, adjudication and appeal. The Secretary of the Commonwealth has the burden of proof, and the trial is conducted as if there were no previous judgments.

Misuse of Commission

Do Not Assist Others with Legal Matters. Notaries follow simple, written rules without having to use significant judgment or discretion. Those who are not attorneys are generally not permitted to assist other persons in drafting, preparing, selecting, completing or understanding a document or transaction.

Exception. Nonattorney Notaries who are specially trained, certified or licensed in a particular field (such as real estate, insurance, escrow, etc.) may advise others about documents in that field, but in no other. In addition, trained paralegals who are not themselves attorneys but are under the supervision of an attorney may advise others about documents in routine legal matters, and this exception applies to paralegals who also are Notaries. In such situations, Notaries should be particularly careful not to transgress any statutes pertaining to disqualifying interest.

Do Not Notarize Own Signature. As a private individual, a Notary may prepare legal documents to which he or she is personally a party, but the Notary may not then notarize his or her signature on these documents. Notaries who overstep their authority by advising others on legal matters may have their appointments revoked and may be prosecuted for the unauthorized practice of law.

Administrative Action

For good cause, the Department may deny, refuse to renew, revoke, suspend, reprimand or impose a condition on a commission for an act or omission which demonstrates that the individual lacks the honesty, integrity, competence or reliability to act as a Notary Public (57 Pa. C.S. 323). ■

Pennsylvania Laws Pertaining to Notaries Public

Reprinted on the following pages are the pertinent parts of the Pennsylvania Statutes affecting Notaries and notarial acts.

TITLE 57. NOTARIES PUBLIC (P. S.)

CHAPTER 2   DUTIES AND POWERS

CHAPTER 3   REVISED UNIFORM LAW ON NOTARIAL ACTS

CHAPTER 2 — DUTIES AND POWERS

57 P. S. § 54d. Acknowledgments and other notarial acts before commissioned officers of armed forces; validation

(a) In addition to the acknowledgement of instruments and the performance of other notarial acts in the manner and form and as otherwise authorized by law, instruments may be acknowledged, documents attested, oaths and affirmations administered, depositions and affidavits executed, and other notarial acts performed, before or by any commissioned officer in active service of the armed forces of the United States with the rank of second lieutenant or higher in the army or marine corps, or with the rank of ensign or higher in the navy or coast guard, or with equivalent rank in any other component part of the armed forces of the United States, by any person who either (a) is a member of the armed forces of the United States, or (b) is a spouse of a member of the armed forces of the United States, or (c) is serving as a merchant seaman outside the limits of the United States included within the forty-eight states and the District of Columbia, or (d) is outside said limits by permission, assignment, or direction of any department or official of the United States Government in connection with any activity pertaining to the prosecution of any war in which the United States is then engaged.

(b) Such acknowledgement of instruments, attestation of documents, administration of oaths and affirmations, execution of depositions and affidavits, and performance of other notarial acts, heretofore or hereafter made or taken, are hereby declared legal, valid and binding; and instruments and documents so acknowledged, authenticated, or sworn to, shall be admissible in evidence and eligible to record in this Commonwealth under the same circumstances and with the same force and effect as if such acknowledgement, attestation, oath, affirmation, deposition, affidavit, or other notarial act had been made or taken within this Commonwealth before or by a duly qualified officer or official as otherwise provided by law.

1953, Aug. 19, P.L. 1104, § 1. Amended 1956, Jan. 31, P.L. (1955) 970, § 1.

CHAPTER 3
REVISED UNIFORM LAW ON NOTARIAL ACTS

Section
301. Short title of chapter.
302. Definitions.
303. Applicability.
304. Authority to perform notarial act.
305. Requirements for certain notarial acts.
306. Personal appearance required.
307. Identification of individual.
308. Authority to refuse to perform notarial act.
309. Signature if individual unable to sign (Reserved).
310. Notarial act in this Commonwealth.
311. Notarial act in another state.
312. Notarial act under authority of federally recognized Indian tribe.
313. Notarial act under Federal authority.
314. Foreign notarial act.
315. Certificate of notarial act.
316. Short form certificates.
317. Official stamp.
318. Stamping device.
319. Journal.
320. Notification regarding performance of notarial act on electronic record; selection of technology.
321. Appointment and commission as notary public; qualifications; no immunity or benefit.
322. Examination, basic education and continuing education.
323. Sanctions.
324. Database of notaries public.
325. Prohibited acts.
326. Validity of notarial acts.

327. Regulations.
328. Notary public commission in effect.
329. Savings clause.
329.1. Fees of notaries public.
330. Uniformity of application and construction.
331. Relation to Electronic Signatures in Global and National Commerce Act.

§ 301. Short title of chapter.

This chapter shall be known and may be cited as the Revised Uniform Law on Notarial Acts.

§ 302. Definitions.

The following words and phrases when used in this chapter shall have the meanings given to them in this section unless the context clearly indicates otherwise:

"Acknowledgment." A declaration by an individual before a notarial officer that:

(1) the individual has signed a record for the purpose stated in the record; and

(2) if the record is signed in a representative capacity, the individual signed the record with proper authority and signed it as the act of the individual or entity identified in the record.

"Bureau." The Bureau of Commissions, Elections and Legislation.

"Conviction." Whether or not judgment of sentence has been imposed, any of the following:

(1) An entry of a plea of guilty or nolo contendere.

(2) A guilty verdict, whether after trial by judge or by jury.

(3) A finding of not guilty due to insanity or of guilty but mentally ill.

"Department." The Department of State of the Commonwealth.

"Electronic." Relating to technology having electrical, digital, magnetic, wireless, optical, electromagnetic or similar capabilities.

"Electronic signature." An electronic symbol, sound or process attached to or logically associated with a record and executed or adopted by an individual with the intent to sign the record.

"In a representative capacity." Acting as:

(1) an authorized officer, agent, partner, trustee or other representative for a person other than an individual;

(2) a public officer, personal representative, guardian or other representative, in the capacity stated in a record;

(3) an agent or attorney-in-fact for a principal; or

(4) an authorized representative of another in any other capacity.

"Notarial act." An act, whether performed with respect to a tangible or electronic record, that a notarial officer may perform under the laws of this Commonwealth. The term includes:

(1) taking an acknowledgment;

(2) administering an oath or affirmation;

(3) taking a verification on oath or affirmation;

(4) witnessing or attesting a signature;

(5) certifying or attesting a copy or deposition; and

(6) noting a protest of a negotiable instrument.

"Notarial officer." A notary public or other individual authorized to perform a notarial act.

"Notary public." An individual commissioned to perform a notarial act by the department.

"Official stamp." A physical image affixed to or embossed on a tangible record or an electronic image attached to or logically associated with an electronic record. The term includes a notary seal.

"Person." Any of the following:

(1) Any individual, corporation, business trust, statutory trust, estate, trust, partnership, limited liability company, association, joint venture or public corporation.

(2) A government or governmental subdivision, agency or instrumentality.

(3) Any other legal or commercial entity.

"Record." Information that is inscribed on a tangible medium or that is stored in an electronic or other medium and is retrievable in perceivable form.

"Recorder of deeds." A county recorder of deeds or an official with similar duties and responsibilities. The term includes the commissioner of records of a county of the first class and the manager of the department of real estate of a county of the second class.

"Secretary." The Secretary of the Commonwealth.

"Sign." With present intent to authenticate or adopt a record:

(1) to execute or adopt a tangible symbol; or

(2) to attach to or logically associate with the record an electronic symbol, sound or process.

"Signature." A tangible symbol or an electronic signature which evidences the signing of a record.

"Stamping device." Any of the following:

(1) A physical device capable of affixing to or embossing on a tangible record an official stamp.

(2) An electronic device or process capable of attaching to or logically associating with an electronic record an official stamp.

"State." A state of the United States, the District of Columbia, Puerto Rico, the Virgin Islands or any territory or insular possession subject to the jurisdiction of the United States.

"Verification on oath or affirmation." A declaration, made by an individual on oath or affirmation before a notarial officer, that a statement in a record is true. The term includes an affidavit.

§ 303. Applicability.

This chapter applies to a notarial act performed on or after the effective date of this chapter.

§ 304. Authority to perform notarial act.

(a) Permitted.--A notarial officer may perform a notarial act authorized by this chapter or by statutory provision other than this chapter.

(b) Prohibited.--

(1) A notarial officer may not perform a notarial act with respect to a

record in which the notarial officer or the notarial officer's spouse has a direct or pecuniary interest.

(2) For the purpose of this subsection, none of the following shall constitute a direct or pecuniary interest:

(i) being a shareholder in a publicly traded company that is a party to the notarized transaction;

(ii) being an officer, director or employee of a company that is a party to the notarized transaction, unless the director, officer or employee personally benefits from the transaction other than as provided under subparagraph (iii); or

(iii) receiving a fee that is not contingent upon the completion of the notarized transaction.

(3) A notarial act performed in violation of this subsection is voidable.

§ 305. Requirements for certain notarial acts.

(a) Acknowledgments.--A notarial officer who takes an acknowledgment of a record shall determine, from personal knowledge or satisfactory evidence of the identity of the individual, all of the following:

(1) The individual appearing before the notarial officer and making the acknowledgment has the identity claimed.

(2) The signature on the record is the signature of the individual.

(b) Verifications.--A notarial officer who takes a verification of a statement on oath or affirmation shall determine, from personal knowledge or satisfactory evidence of the identity of the individual, all of the following:

(1) The individual appearing before the notarial officer and making the verification has the identity claimed.

(2) The signature on the statement verified is the signature of the individual.

(c) Signatures.--A notarial officer who witnesses or attests to a signature shall determine, from personal knowledge or satisfactory evidence of the identity of the individual, all of the following:

(1) The individual appearing before the notarial officer and signing the record has the identity claimed.

(2) The signature on the record is the signature of the individual.

(d) Copies.--A notarial officer who certifies or attests a copy of a record or an item which was copied shall determine that the copy is a complete and accurate transcription or reproduction of the record or item.

(e) Negotiable instruments.--A notarial officer who makes or notes a protest of a negotiable instrument shall determine the matters set forth in 13 Pa.C.S. § 3505(b) (relating to evidence of dishonor).

§ 306. Personal appearance required.

If a notarial act relates to a statement made in or a signature executed on a record, the individual making the statement or executing the signature shall appear personally before the notarial officer.

§ 307. Identification of individual.

(a) Personal knowledge.--A notarial officer has personal knowledge of the identity of an individual appearing before the notarial officer if the individual is personally known to the notarial officer through dealings sufficient to provide reasonable certainty that the individual has the identity claimed.

(b) Satisfactory evidence.--A notarial officer has satisfactory evidence of the identity of an individual appearing before the notarial officer if the notarial officer can identify the individual as set forth in any of the following paragraphs:

(1) By means set forth in any of the following subparagraphs:

(i) A passport, driver's license or government-issued nondriver identification card, which is current and unexpired.

(ii) Another form of government identification issued to an individual, which:

(A) is current;

(B) contains the signature or a photograph of the individual; and

(C) is satisfactory to the notarial officer.

(2) By a verification on oath or affirmation of a credible witness personally appearing before the notarial officer and personally known to the notarial officer.

(c) Discretion.--A notarial officer may require an individual to provide additional information or identification credentials necessary to assure the notarial officer of the identity of the individual.

§ 308. Authority to refuse to perform notarial act.

(a) Specific refusal.--A notarial officer may refuse to perform a notarial act if the notarial officer is not satisfied that:

(1) the individual executing the record is competent or has the capacity to execute the record;

(2) the individual's signature is knowingly and voluntarily made;

(3) the individual's signature on the record or statement substantially conforms to the signature on a form of identification used to determine the identity of the individual; or

(4) the physical appearance of the individual signing the record or statement substantially conforms to the photograph on a form of identification used to determine the identity of the individual.

(b) General refusal.--A notarial officer may refuse to perform a notarial act unless refusal is prohibited by law other than this chapter.

§ 309. Signature if individual unable to sign (Reserved).

§ 310. Notarial act in this Commonwealth.

(a) Eligible individuals.--A notarial act may be performed in this Commonwealth by any of the following:

(1) A judge of a court of record.

(2) A clerk, prothonotary or deputy prothonotary or deputy clerk of a court having a seal.

(3) Any of the following:

(i) A recorder of deeds.

(ii) A deputy recorder of deeds.

(iii) A clerk of a recorder of deeds to the extent authorized by:

(A) section 1 of the act of May 17, 1949 (P.L.1397, No.414), entitled "An act authorizing the recorder of deeds in counties of the first class to appoint and empower clerks employed in his office to administer oaths and affirmations";

(B) section 1312 of the act of July 28, 1953 (P.L.723, No.230), known as the Second Class County Code; or

(C) section 1313 of the act of August 9, 1955 (P.L.323, No.130), known as The County Code.

(4) A notary public.

(5) A member of the minor judiciary. As used in this paragraph, the term "minor judiciary" has the meaning given in 42 Pa.C.S. § 102 (relating to definitions).

(6) An individual authorized by law to perform a specific notarial act.

(b) Prima facie evidence.--The signature and title of an individual performing a notarial act in this Commonwealth are prima facie evidence that:

(1) the signature is genuine; and

(2) the individual holds the designated title.

(c) Conclusive determination.--The signature and title of a notarial officer described in subsection (a)(1), (2), (3), (4) or (5) conclusively establish the authority of the notarial officer to perform the notarial act.

§ 311. Notarial act in another state.

(a) Effect.--A notarial act performed in another state has the same effect under the law of this Commonwealth as if performed by a notarial officer of this Commonwealth if the act performed in that state is performed by any of the following:

(1) A notary public of that state.

(2) A judge, clerk or deputy clerk of a court of that state.

(3) An individual authorized by the law of that state to perform the notarial act.

(b) Prima facie evidence.--The signature and title of an individual performing a notarial act in another state are prima facie evidence that:

(1) the signature is genuine; and

(2) the individual holds the designated title.

(c) Conclusive determination.--The signature and title of a notarial officer described in subsection (a)(1) or (2) conclusively establish the authority of the notarial officer to perform the notarial act.

§ 312. Notarial act under authority of federally recognized Indian tribe.

(a) Effect.--A notarial act performed under the authority and in the jurisdiction of a federally recognized Indian tribe has the same effect as if performed by a notarial officer of this Commonwealth if the act performed in the jurisdiction of the tribe is performed by any of the following:

(1) A notary public of the tribe.

(2) A judge, clerk or deputy clerk of a court of the tribe.

(3) An individual authorized by the law of the tribe to perform the notarial act.

(b) Prima facie evidence.--The signature and title of an individual performing a notarial act under the authority of and in the jurisdiction of a federally recognized Indian tribe are prima facie evidence that:

(1) the signature is genuine; and

(2) the individual holds the designated title.

(c) Conclusive determination.--The signature and title of a notarial officer described in subsection (a)(1) or (2) conclusively establish the authority of the notarial officer to perform the notarial act.

§ 313. Notarial act under Federal authority.

(a) Effect.--A notarial act performed under Federal law has the same effect under the law of this Commonwealth as if performed by a notarial officer of this Commonwealth if the act performed under Federal law is performed by any of the following:

(1) A judge, clerk or deputy clerk of a court.

(2) An individual in military service or performing duties under the authority of military service who is authorized to perform notarial acts under Federal law.

(3) An individual designated a notarizing officer by the United States Department of State for performing notarial acts overseas.

(4) An individual authorized by Federal law to perform the notarial act.

(b) Prima facie evidence.--The signature and title of an individual acting under Federal authority and performing a notarial act are prima facie evidence that:

(1) the signature is genuine; and

(2) the individual holds the designated title.

(c) Conclusive determination.--The signature and title of a notarial officer described in subsection (a)(1), (2) or (3) conclusively establish the authority of the notarial officer to perform the notarial act.

§ 314. Foreign notarial act.

(a) (Reserved).

(b) Effect.--

(1) This subsection applies to a notarial act:

(i) performed under authority and in the jurisdiction of a foreign state or constituent unit of the foreign state; or

(ii) performed under the authority of a multinational or international governmental organization.

(2) A notarial act under paragraph (1) has the same effect under the law of this Commonwealth as if performed by a notarial officer of this Commonwealth.

(c) Conclusive establishment.--If the title of office and indication of authority to perform notarial acts in a foreign state appears in a digest of foreign law or in a list customarily used as a source for that information, the authority of an officer with that title to perform notarial acts is conclusively established.

(d) Prima facie evidence.--The signature and official stamp of an individual holding an office described in subsection (c) are prima facie evidence that:

(1) the signature is genuine; and

(2) the individual holds the designated title.

(e) Hague Convention.--

(1) This subsection applies to an apostille which is:

(i) in the form prescribed by the Hague Convention of October 5, 1961; and

(ii) issued by a foreign state party to the Hague Convention.

(2) An apostille under paragraph (1) conclusively establishes that:

(i) the signature of the notarial officer is genuine; and
(ii) the notarial officer holds the indicated office.
(f) Consular authentications.--
(1) This subsection applies to a consular authentication:
(i) issued by an individual designated by the United States Department of State as a notarizing officer for performing notarial acts overseas; and
(ii) attached to the record with respect to which the notarial act is performed.
(2) A consular authentication under paragraph (1) conclusively establishes that:
(i) the signature of the notarial officer is genuine; and
(ii) the notarial officer holds the indicated office.
(g) Definition.--As used in this section, the term "foreign state" means a government other than the United States, a state or a federally recognized Indian tribe.

§ 315. Certificate of notarial act.

(a) Requirements.--
(1) A notarial act shall be evidenced by a certificate.
(2) Regardless of whether the notarial officer is a notary public, the certificate must:
(i) be executed contemporaneously with the performance of the notarial act;
(ii) be signed and dated by the notarial officer;
(iii) identify the county and State in which the notarial act is performed; and
(iv) contain the title of office of the notarial officer.
(3) If the notarial officer is a notary public, all of the following subparagraphs apply:
(i) The notary public must:
(A) sign the notary public's name exactly and only as it appears on the commission; or
(B) execute the notary public's electronic signature in a manner which attributes the signature to the notary public identified in the commission.
(ii) The certificate must indicate the date of expiration of the notarial officer's commission.
(b) Official stamp.--
(1) If a notarial act regarding a tangible record is performed by a notary public, an official stamp shall be affixed to the certificate near the notary public's signature in a form capable of photographic reproduction.
(2) If a notarial act is performed regarding a tangible record by a notarial officer other than a notary public and the certificate contains the information specified in subsection (a)(2)(ii), (iii) and (iv), an official stamp may be affixed to the certificate.
(3) If a notarial act regarding an electronic record is performed by a notary public and the certificate contains the information specified in subsection (a)(2)(ii), (iii) and (iv) and (3), an official stamp may be attached to or logically associated with the certificate.
(4) If a notarial act regarding an electronic record is performed by a

notarial officer other than a notary public and the certificate contains the information specified in subsection (a)(2)(ii), (iii) and (iv), an official stamp may be attached to or logically associated with the certificate.

(c) Sufficiency.--A certificate of a notarial act is sufficient if it meets the requirements of subsections (a) and (b) and:

(1) is in a short form set forth in section 316 (relating to short form certificates);

(2) is in a form otherwise permitted by a statutory provision;

(3) is in a form permitted by the law applicable in the jurisdiction in which the notarial act was performed; or

(4) sets forth the actions of the notarial officer and the actions are sufficient to meet the requirements of the notarial act as provided in:

(i) sections 305 (relating to requirements for certain notarial acts), 306 (relating to personal appearance required) and 307 (relating to identification of individual); or

(ii) a statutory provision other than this chapter.

(d) Effect.--By executing a certificate of a notarial act, a notarial officer certifies that the notarial officer has complied with the requirements and made the determinations specified in sections 304 (relating to authority to perform notarial act), 305 and 306.

(e) Prohibition.--A notarial officer may not affix the notarial officer's signature to or logically associate it with a certificate until the notarial act has been performed.

(f) Process.--

(1) If a notarial act is performed regarding a tangible record, a certificate shall be part of or securely attached to the record.

(2) If a notarial act is performed regarding an electronic record, the certificate shall be affixed to or logically associated with the electronic record.

(3) If the department has established standards under section 327 (relating to regulations) for attaching, affixing or logically associating the certificate, the process must conform to the standards.

§ 316. Short form certificates.

The following short form certificates of notarial acts are sufficient for the purposes indicated if completed with the information required by section 315(a) and (b) (relating to certificate of notarial act):

(1) For an acknowledgment in an individual capacity:

State of
County of

This record was acknowledged before me on _____ (date) by _____(name(s) of individual(s))

Signature of notarial officer
Stamp
Title of office
My commission expires:

(2) For an acknowledgment in a representative capacity:

State of
County of

This record was acknowledged before me on _____ (date) by _____(name(s) of individual(s)) as _____(type of authority, such as officer or trustee) who represent that (he, she or they) are authorized to act on behalf of _____ (name of party on behalf of whom record was executed)

Signature of notarial officer
Stamp
Title of office
My commission expires:

(2.1) For an acknowledgment by an attorney at law (relating to oaths and acknowledgments):

State of
County of

This record was acknowledged before me on _____ (date) by _____ (name of attorney)
Supreme Court identification number _____
as a member of the bar of the Pennsylvania Supreme Court and a subscribing witness to this record and certified that he/she was personally present when _____ (name(s) of individual(s)) executed the record and that _____ (name(s) of individual(s)) executed the record for the purposes contained therein.

Signature of notarial officer
Stamp
Title of office
My commission expires:

(3) For a verification on oath or affirmation:

State of
County of
Signed and sworn to (or affirmed) before me on _____ (date) by _____ (name(s) of individual(s))
making statement _____
_____

Signature of notarial officer
Stamp
Title of office
My commission expires:

(4) For witnessing or attesting a signature:

State of

County of

Signed (or attested) before me on _____ (date)
by _____ (name(s) of individual(s))

Signature of notarial officer
Stamp
Title of office
My commission expires:

(5) For certifying a copy of a record:

State of
County of

I certify that this is a true and correct copy of a _____
in the possession of _____
Dated

Signature of notarial officer
Stamp
Title of office
My commission expires:

(6) For certifying the transcript of a deposition:

State of
County of

I certify that this is a true and correct copy of the transcript of the deposition of _____
Dated

Signature of notarial officer
Stamp
Title of office:
My commission expires:

§ 317. Official stamp.

The following shall apply to the official stamp of a notary public:

(1) A notary public shall provide and keep an official seal, which shall be used to authenticate all the acts, instruments and attestations of the notary public. The seal must be a rubber stamp and must show clearly in the following order:

(i) The words "Commonwealth of Pennsylvania."

(ii) The words "Notary Seal."

(iii) The name as it appears on the commission of the notary public and the words "Notary Public."

(iv) The name of the county in which the notary public maintains an office.

(v) The date the notary public's commission expires.

(vi) Any other information required by the department.

(2) The seal must have a maximum height of one inch and width of three and one-half inches, with a plain border.

(3) The seal must be capable of being copied together with the record to which it is affixed or attached or with which it is logically associated.

§ 318. Stamping device.

(a) Security.--

(1) A notary public is responsible for the security of the stamping device of the notary public. A notary public may not allow another individual to use the device to perform a notarial act.

(2) On resignation of a notary public commission or on the expiration of the date set forth in the stamping device, the notary public shall disable the stamping device by destroying, defacing, damaging, erasing or securing it against use in a manner which renders it unusable.

(2.1) An individual whose notary public commission has been suspended or revoked shall surrender possession of the stamping device to the department.

(3) On the death or adjudication of incompetency of a notary public, the personal representative or guardian of the notary public or any person knowingly in possession of the stamping device shall render it unusable by destroying, defacing, damaging, erasing or securing it against use in a manner which renders it unusable.

(b) Loss or theft.--If a stamping device is lost or stolen, the notary public or the personal representative or guardian of the notary public shall notify the department promptly upon discovering that the device is lost or stolen.

§ 319. Journal.

(a) Maintenance.--A notary public shall maintain a journal in which the notary public records in chronological order all notarial acts that the notary public performs.

(b) Format.--A journal may be created on a tangible medium or in an electronic format. A notary public may maintain a separate journal for tangible records and for electronic records. If the journal is maintained on a tangible medium, it shall be a bound register with numbered pages. If the journal is maintained in an electronic format, it shall be in a tamper-evident electronic format complying with the regulations of the department.

(c) Entries.--An entry in a journal shall be made contemporaneously with performance of the notarial act and contain all of the following information:

(1) The date and time of the notarial act.

(2) A description of the record, if any, and type of notarial act.

(3) The full name and address of each individual for whom the notarial act is performed.

(4) If identity of the individual is based on personal knowledge, a statement to that effect.

(5) If identity of the individual is based on satisfactory evidence, a brief description of the method of identification and any identification credential presented, including the date of issuance and expiration of an identification credential.

(6) The fee charged by the notary public.

(d) Loss or theft.--If a journal is lost or stolen, the notary public shall promptly notify the department on discovering that the journal is lost or stolen.

(e) Termination of office.--A notary public shall deliver the journal of the notary public to the office of the recorder of deeds in the county where the notary public last maintained an office within 30 days of:

(1) expiration of the commission of the notary public, unless the notary public applies for a commission within that time period;

(2) resignation of the commission of the notary public; or

(3) revocation of the commission of the notary public.

(f) Repository.--(Reserved).

(g) Death or incompetency.--On the death or adjudication of incompetency of a current or former notary public, the personal representative or guardian of the notary public or a person knowingly in possession of the journal of the notary public shall deliver it within 30 days to the office of the recorder of deeds in the county where the notary public last maintained an office.

(g.1) Certified copies.--A notary public shall give a certified copy of the journal to a person that applies for it.

(h) Protection.--

(1) A journal and each public record of the notary public are exempt from execution.

(2) A journal is the exclusive property of the notary public.

(3) A journal may not be:

(i) used by any person other than the notary public; or

(ii) surrendered to an employer of the notary public upon termination of employment.

§ 320. Notification regarding performance of notarial act on electronic record; selection of technology.

(a) Selection.--A notary public may select one or more tamper-evident technologies to perform notarial acts with respect to electronic records. A person may not require a notary public to perform a notarial act with respect to an electronic record with a technology that the notary public has not selected.

(b) Notice and approval.--

(1) Before a notary public performs the initial notarial act with respect to an electronic record, a notary public shall notify the department that the notary public will be performing notarial acts with respect to electronic records and identify each technology the notary public intends to use.

(2) If the department has established standards for approval of technology under section 327 (relating to regulations), the technology must conform to the standards. If the technology conforms to the standards, the department shall approve the use of the technology.

§ 321. Appointment and commission as notary public; qualifications; no immunity or benefit.

(a) Eligibility.--An applicant for appointment and commission as a notary public must meet all of the following:

(1) Be at least 18 years of age.

(2) Be a citizen or permanent legal resident of the United States.

PENNSYLVANIA NOTARY PRIMER

(3) Be a resident of or have a place of employment or practice in this Commonwealth.

(4) Be able to read and write English.

(5) Not be disqualified to receive a commission under section 323 (relating to sanctions).

(6) Have passed the examination required under section 322(a) (relating to examination, basic education and continuing education).

(7) Comply with other requirements established by the department by regulation as necessary to insure the competence, integrity and qualifications of a notary public and to insure the proper performance of notarial acts.

(b) Application.--An individual qualified under subsection (a) may apply to the department for appointment and commission as a notary public. The application must comply with all of the following:

(1) Be made to the department on a form prescribed by the department.

(2) Be accompanied by a nonrefundable fee of $42, payable to the Commonwealth of Pennsylvania. This amount shall include the application fee for notary public commission and fee for filing of the bond with the department.

(3) (Deleted by amendment.)

(c) Oath or affirmation.--Upon appointment and before issuance of a commission as a notary public, an applicant must execute an oath or affirmation of office.

(d) Bond.--

(1) Within 45 days after appointment and before issuance of a commission as a notary public, the applicant must obtain a surety bond in:

(i) the amount of $10,000; or

(ii) the amount set by regulation of the department.

(2) (Reserved).

(3) The bond must:

(i) be executed by an insurance company authorized to do business in this Commonwealth;

(ii) cover acts performed during the term of the notary public commission; and

(iii) be in the form prescribed by the department.

(4) If a notary public violates law with respect to notaries public in this Commonwealth, the surety or issuing entity is liable under the bond.

(5) The surety or issuing entity must give 30 days' notice to the department before canceling the bond.

(6) The surety or issuing entity shall notify the department not later than 30 days after making a payment to a claimant under the bond.

(7) A notary public may perform notarial acts in this Commonwealth only during the period in which a valid bond is on file with the department.

(d.1) Official signature.--

(1) The official signature of each notary public shall be registered, for a fee of 50¢, in the "Notary Register" provided for that purpose in the prothonotary's office of the county where the notary public maintains an office within:

(i) 45 days after appointment or reappointment; and

(ii) 30 days after moving to a different county.

(2) In a county of the second class, the official signature of each notary public shall be registered in the office of the clerk of courts within the time periods specified in paragraph (1).

(d.2) Recording and filing.--

(1) Upon appointment and prior to entering into the duties of a notary public, the bond, oath of office and commission must be recorded in the office of the recorder of deeds of the county in which the notary public maintains an office.

(2) Upon reappointment, the bond, oath of office and commission must be recorded in the office of the recorder of deeds of the county in which the notary public maintains an office.

(3) Within 90 days of recording under this subsection, a copy of the bond and oath of office must be filed with the department.

(e) Issuance.--On compliance with this section, the department shall issue to an applicant a commission as a notary public for a term of four years.

(f) Effect.--

(1) A commission to act as a notary public authorizes a notary public to perform notarial acts. If a notary public fails to comply with subsection (d.1) or (d.2), the notary public's commission shall be null and void.

(2) A commission to act as a notary public does not provide a notary public any immunity or benefit conferred by law of this Commonwealth on public officials or employees.

§ 322. Examination, basic education and continuing education.

(a) Examination.--An applicant for a commission as a notary public who does not hold a commission in this Commonwealth must pass an examination administered by the department or an entity approved by the department. The examination must be based on the course of study described in subsection (b).

(b) Basic education.--An applicant under subsection (a) must, within the six-month period immediately preceding application, complete a course of at least three hours of notary public basic education approved by the department. For approval, the following apply:

(1) The course must cover the statutes, regulations, procedures and ethics relevant to notarial acts, with a core curriculum including the duties and responsibilities of the office of notary public and electronic notarization.

(2) The course must either be interactive or classroom instruction.

(c) Continuing education.--An applicant for renewal of appointment and commission as a notary public must, within the six-month period immediately preceding application, complete a course of at least three hours of notary public continuing education approved by the department. For approval, the following apply:

(1) The course must cover topics which ensure maintenance and enhancement of skill, knowledge and competency necessary to perform notarial acts.

(2) The course must either be interactive or classroom instruction.

(d) Preapproval.--All basic and continuing education courses of study must be preapproved by the department.

§ 323. Sanctions.

(a) Authority.--The department may deny, refuse to renew, revoke, suspend, reprimand or impose a condition on a commission as notary public for an act or omission which demonstrates that the individual lacks the honesty, integrity, competence or reliability to act as a notary public. Such acts or omissions include:

(1) Failure to comply with this chapter.

(2) A fraudulent, dishonest or deceitful misstatement or omission in the application for a commission as a notary public submitted to the department.

(3) Conviction of or acceptance of Accelerated Rehabilitative Disposition by the applicant or notary public for a felony or an offense involving fraud, dishonesty or deceit.

(4) A finding against or admission of liability by the applicant or notary public in a legal proceeding or disciplinary action based on the fraud, dishonesty or deceit of the applicant or notary public.

(5) Failure by a notary public to discharge a duty required of a notary public, whether by this chapter, by regulation of the department or by Federal or State law.

(6) Use of false or misleading advertising or representation by a notary public representing that the notary public has a duty, right or privilege that the notary public does not have.

(7) Violation by a notary public of a regulation of the department regarding a notary public.

(8) Denial, refusal to renew, revocation, suspension or conditioning of a notary public commission in another state.

(9) Failure of a notary public to maintain a bond under section 321(d) (relating to appointment and commission as notary public; qualifications; no immunity or benefit).

(a.1) Administrative penalty.--The department may impose an administrative penalty of up to $1,000 on a notary public for each act or omission which constitutes a violation of this chapter or on any person who performs a notarial act without being properly appointed and commissioned under this chapter.

(b) Administrative Agency Law.--Action by the department under subsection (a) or (a.1) is subject to 2 Pa.C.S. Chs. 5 Subch. A (relating to practice and procedure of Commonwealth agencies) and 7 Subch. A (relating to judicial review of Commonwealth agency action).

(c) Other remedies.--The authority of the department under this section does not prevent a person from seeking and obtaining other criminal or civil remedies provided by law.

(d) Investigations and hearings.--

(1) The department may issue a subpoena, upon application of an attorney responsible for representing the Commonwealth in disciplinary matters before the department, for the purpose of investigating alleged violations of the disciplinary provisions administered by the department.

(2) In an investigation or hearing, the department, as it deems necessary, may subpoena witnesses, administer oaths, examine witnesses, take testimony and compel the production of documents.

(3) The department may apply to Commonwealth Court under 42 Pa.C.S. § 761(a)(2) (relating to original jurisdiction) to enforce a subpoena under this subsection.

(e) Other enforcement authority.--The department may initiate civil proceedings at law or in equity to enforce the requirements of this chapter and to enforce regulations or orders issued under this chapter. In addition, the department may request the prosecution of criminal offenses to the extent provided by this chapter or as otherwise provided by law relating to notaries public, notarial officers or notarial acts, in the manner provided by the act of October 15, 1980 (P.L.950, No.164), known as the Commonwealth Attorneys Act.

(f) Criminal penalties applicable.--The following apply:

(1) Except as provided in this chapter or otherwise provided by law, it is unlawful for a person to hold himself out as a notary public or as a notarial officer or to perform a notarial act.

(2) Falsely pretending to be a notary public or a notarial officer and performing any action in furtherance of such false pretense shall subject the person to the penalties set forth in 18 Pa.C.S. § 4913 (relating to impersonating a notary public or a holder of a professional or occupational license).

(3) The use of an official stamp by a person who is not a notary public named on the stamp shall constitute a violation of 18 Pa.C.S. § 4913.

(4) Except as provided in paragraph (2) or (3), any person violating this chapter or a regulation of the department commits a summary offense and shall, upon conviction, be sentenced to pay a fine of not more than $1,000.

§ 324. Database of notaries public.

The department shall maintain an electronic database of notaries public:

(1) through which a person may verify the authority of a notary public to perform notarial acts; and

(2) which indicates whether a notary public has notified the department that the notary public will be performing notarial acts on electronic records.

§ 325. Prohibited acts.

(a) No authority.--A commission as a notary public does not authorize the notary public to:

(1) assist persons in drafting legal records, give legal advice or otherwise practice law;

(2) act as an immigration consultant or an expert on immigration matters;

(3) represent a person in a judicial or administrative proceeding relating to immigration to the United States, United States citizenship or related matters; or

(4) receive compensation for performing any of the activities listed in this subsection.

(b) False advertising.--A notary public may not engage in false or deceptive advertising.

(c) Designation.--

(1) Except as set forth in paragraph (2), a notary public may not use the term "notario" or "notario publico."
(2) Paragraph (1) does not apply to an attorney at law.
(d) Representations.--
(1) Except as set forth in paragraph (2), the following apply:
(i) A notary public may not advertise or represent that the notary public may:
(A) assist persons in drafting legal records;
(B) give legal advice; or
(C) otherwise practice law.
(ii) If a notary public advertises or represents that the notary public offers notarial services, whether orally or in a record, including broadcast media, print media and the Internet, the notary public shall include the following statement, or an alternate statement authorized or required by the department, in the advertisement or representation, prominently and in each language used in the advertisement or representation:
I am not an attorney licensed to practice law in this Commonwealth. I am not allowed to draft legal records, give advice on legal matters, including immigration, or charge a fee for those activities.
(iii) If the form of advertisement or representation is not broadcast media, print media or the Internet and does not permit inclusion of the statement required by this subsection because of size, it shall be displayed prominently or provided at the place of performance of the notarial act before the notarial act is performed.
(2) Paragraph (1) does not apply to an attorney at law.
(e) Original records.--Except as otherwise allowed by law, a notary public may not withhold access to or possession of an original record provided by a person that seeks performance of a notarial act by the notary public.
(f) Crimes Code.--There are provisions in 18 Pa.C.S. (relating to crimes and offenses) which apply to notaries public.

§ 326. Validity of notarial acts.

(a) Failures.--Except as otherwise provided in section 304(b) (relating to authority to perform notarial act), the failure of a notarial officer to perform a duty or meet a requirement specified in this chapter does not invalidate a notarial act performed by the notarial officer.
(b) Invalidation.--The validity of a notarial act under this chapter does not prevent an aggrieved person from seeking to invalidate the record or transaction which is the subject of the notarial act or from seeking other remedies based on Federal law or the law of this Commonwealth other than this chapter.
(c) Lack of authority.--This section does not validate a purported notarial act performed by an individual who does not have the authority to perform notarial acts.

§ 327. Regulations.

(a) Authority.--Except as provided in section 329.1(a)(relating to fees of notaries public), the department may promulgate regulations to implement this chapter. Regulations regarding the performance of notarial acts with respect to electronic records may not require or accord greater legal status or effect to the implementation or application of a specific technology or technical specification. Regulations may:

(1) Prescribe the manner of performing notarial acts regarding tangible and electronic records.

(2) Include provisions to ensure that any change to or tampering with a record bearing a certificate of a notarial act is self-evident.

(3) Include provisions to ensure integrity in the creation, transmittal, storage or authentication of electronic records or signatures.

(4) Prescribe the process of granting, renewing, conditioning, denying, suspending or revoking a notary public commission and assuring the trustworthiness of an individual holding a commission as notary public.

(5) Include provisions to prevent fraud or mistake in the performance of notarial acts.

(6) Establish the process for approving and accepting surety bonds under section 321(d) (relating to appointment and commission as notary public; qualifications; no immunity or benefit).

(7) Provide for the administration of the examination under section 322(a) (relating to examination, basic education and continuing education) and the course of study under section 322(b).

(7.1) Require applicants for appointment and commission as notaries public to submit criminal history record information as provided in 18 Pa.C.S. Ch. 91 (relating to criminal history record information) as a condition of appointment.

(8) Include any other provision necessary to implement this chapter.

(b) Considerations.--In promulgating regulations about notarial acts with respect to electronic records, the department shall consider, so far as is consistent with this chapter:

(1) the most recent standards regarding electronic records promulgated by national bodies, such as the National Association of Secretaries of State;

(2) standards, practices and customs of other states which substantially enact the Revised Uniform Law on Notarial Acts; and

(3) the views of governmental officials and entities and other interested persons.

§ 328. Notary public commission in effect.

A commission as a notary public in effect on the effective date of this chapter continues until its date of expiration. A notary public who applies to renew a commission as a notary public on or after the effective date of this chapter is subject to this chapter. A notary public, in performing notarial acts after the effective date of this chapter, shall comply with this chapter.

§ 329. Savings clause.

This chapter does not affect the validity or effect of a notarial act performed before the effective date of this chapter.

§ 329.1. Fees of notaries public.

(a) Department.--The fees of notaries public shall be fixed by the department by regulation.

(b) Prohibition.--A notary public may not charge or receive a notary public fee in excess of the fee fixed by the department.

(c) Operation.--

(1) The fees of the notary public shall be separately stated.

(2) A notary public may waive the right to charge a fee.

(3) Unless paragraph (2) applies, a notary public shall:

(i) display fees in a conspicuous location in the place of business of the notary public; or

(ii) provide fees, upon request, to a person utilizing the services of the notary public.

(d) Presumption.--The fee for a notary public:

(1) shall be the property of the notary public; and

(2) unless mutually agreed by the notary public and the employer, shall not belong to or be received by the entity that employs the notary public.

§ 330. Uniformity of application and construction.

In applying and construing this chapter, consideration must be given to the need to promote uniformity of the law with respect to its subject matter among states that enact it.

§ 331. Relation to Electronic Signatures in Global and National Commerce Act.

To the extent permitted by section 102 of the Electronic Signatures in Global and National Commerce Act (Public Law 106-229, 15 U.S.C. § 7002), this chapter may modify or supersede provisions of that act.

2013, Oct. 9, P.L. 609, No. 73, § 2, effective 180 days after published notice of 57 Pa.C.S.A. § 322 course approval. Amended 2014, July 9, P.L. 1035, No. 119, § 1, effective 180 days after published notice of 57 Pa.C.S.A. § 322 course approval.

The remaining sections of Act 73:

Section 3. Repeals are as follows:

(1) The General Assembly declares that the repeals under paragraph (2) are necessary to effectuate the addition of 57 Pa.C.S. Ch. 3.

(2) The following acts and parts of acts are repealed:

(i) The act of May 24, 1917 (P.L.270, No.147), entitled "An act to validate affidavits, acknowledgments, and other notarial acts, heretofore performed by notaries public of this Commonwealth within three months after the expiration of the time for which they have been commissioned to act."

(ii) The act of March 14, 1919 (P.L.18, No.9), entitled "An act conferring upon judge advocates of the United States Army the powers of notaries public, declaring the effect thereof; validating notarial acts heretofore performed by judge advocates, and declaring the effect thereof."

(iii) Section 618-A(1)(i) of the act of April 9, 1929 (P.L.177, No.175), known as The Administrative Code of 1929.

(iv) The act of June 1, 1933 (P.L.1150, No.286), entitled "A supplement to an act, approved May sixth, one thousand nine hundred and thirty-one (Pamphlet Laws, ninety-nine), entitled 'An act to amend section seven of the act, approved the fifth day of March, one thousand seven hundred and ninety-one (three Smith's Laws, six), entitled "An act to enable the Governor to appoint Notaries Public, and for other purposes therein mentioned," prescribing the form of notary seal,' by providing that the presence of the arms of this Commonwealth on the seal of a notary public reappointed after the effective date of the act to which this is a supplement, and prior to the effective date of this act, shall not invalidate said seal, or the notarial acts, instruments or attestations authenticated by such seal."

(v) The act of May 25, 1939 (P.L.223, No.125), entitled "An act relating to the administration of oaths, by notaries public, magistrates, alderman and justices of the peace; and validating certain oaths heretofore taken."

(vi) The act of July 24, 1941 (P.L.490, No.188), known as the Uniform Acknowledgment Act.

(vii) The act of July 28, 1953 (P.L.676, No.211), entitled "An act authorizing acknowledgments and affidavits by persons on active duty with the armed forces of the United States before persons authorized by act of Congress to act as notaries public; and validating certain acknowledgments and affidavits."

(viii) The act of August 19, 1953 (P.L.1104, No.301), entitled "An act relating to the acknowledgment of instruments, the attestation of documents, the administration of oaths and affirmations, the execution of depositions and affidavits, and other notarial acts, heretofore or hereafter taken before any commissioned officer of the armed forces of the United States, and providing that such instruments and documents executed by any person who is a member of or actually present with the armed forces of the United States or is outside the United States for certain purposes shall be legal, valid and binding, and providing for the form of the instrument or document and what proof shall be sufficient of the authority of such commissioned officer so to act."

(ix) The act of August 21, 1953 (P.L.1323, No.373), known as The Notary Public Law.

(x) The act of December 13, 1955 (P.L.848, No.251), entitled "An act providing for the revocation of commission of notaries public issuing checks without funds on deposit."

Section 3.1. The fee of $25 for a Notary Public Commission and the $2 fee for Filing Bond for any Public Office in 4 Pa. Code § 161.1 are abrogated.

Section 4. Upon approval of courses under 57 Pa.C.S. § 322(b) and (c), the Department of State shall transmit notice of the approval to the Legislative Reference Bureau for publication in the Pennsylvania Bulletin.

Section 5. This act shall take effect as follows:

(1) The following provisions shall take effect immediately:

(i) The authority of the Department of State to approve courses under 57 Pa.C.S. § 322(b) and (c).

(ii) The addition of 57 Pa.C.S. §§ 327 and 329.1(a).

(iii) Section 4 of this act.

(iv) This section.

(2) The addition of 42 Pa.C.S. Ch. 62 shall take effect in 60 days.

(3) The remainder of this act shall take effect 180 days after publication of the notice under section 4 of this act.

NOTARY PUBLIC FEE SCHEDULE
AS OF MAY 28, 2005
THE SECRETARY OF THE COMMONWEALTH
REVISED NOTARY FEES

Executing affidavits (no matter how many signatures).....................$5.00
Executing acknowledgments 5.00
    in executing acknowledgments, each additional name 2.00
Executing certificates (per certified copy) 5.00
Administering oaths (per individual taking an oath)..........................5.00
Taking depositions (per page) 3.00
Executing verifications
Executing protests (per page) 3.00
    1953, Aug. 21, P.L. 1323, § 21. Amended 2002, Dec. 9, P.L. 1269, No. 151, § 10, effective July 1, 2003; Amended 2005, effective May 28, 2005.

TITLE 21. DEEDS AND MORTGAGES (P. S.)
CHAPTER 1. DEEDS AND GENERAL PROVISIONS
EXECUTION, PROBATE AND ACKNOWLEDGMENT
GENERAL PROVISIONS

21 P. S. § 42. Deeds to be acknowledged before recording

All bargains and sales, deeds and conveyances of lands, tenements and hereditaments, in this province, may be recorded in the said office; but before the same shall be so recorded, the parties concerned shall procure the grantor or bargainer named in every such deed, or else two or more of the witnesses (who were present at the execution thereof), to come before one of the justices of the peace of the proper county or city where the lands lie, who is hereby empowered to take such acknowledgment of the grantor, if one, or of one of the grantors, if more.

The "office for recording of deeds" established by section 1 of the act (section 3241 of Title 16, Counties).

1715, May 28, 1 Sm.L. 94, § 2.

21 P. S. § 43. Proof of execution where grantor is dead or cannot appear

But in the case the grantor be dead, or cannot appear, then the witnesses brought before such justice shall by him be examined upon oath or affirmation, to prove the execution of the deed then produced. Whereupon the same justice shall, under his hand and seal, certify such acknowledgment or proof upon the back of the deed, with the day and year when the same was made, and by whom; and that after the recorder has recorded any of the said deeds, he shall certify on the back thereof, under his hand and seal of his office, the day he entered it, and the name or number of the book or roll, and page, where the same is entered.

1715, May 28, 1 Sm.L. 94, § 3.

21 P. S. § 44. Proof of deeds where grantor and witnesses are dead or cannot be found

PENNSYLVANIA LAWS PERTAINING TO NOTARIES PUBLIC

Whereas there is no provision made by the act, to which this is a supplement, for the proving deeds or conveyances where the grantors and the witnesses are deceased; for remedy whereof, Be it enacted, That from and after the publication of this act, where the grantors and witnesses of any deed or conveyance are deceased, or cannot be had, it shall and may be lawful to and for any of the justices of the supreme court, or any justice of the court of common pleas of the county where the lands lie, to take the examination of any witness or witnesses, on oath or affirmation, to prove the handwriting of such deceased witness or witnesses, or where such proof cannot be had, then to prove the handwriting of the grantor or grantors, which shall be certified by the justice before whom such proof shall be made, and such deed or conveyance, being so proved, shall be recorded as is usual in other cases directed by the said act.

Act of 1715, May 28, 1 Sm.L. 94 (incorporated in this title and Title 16, Counties). 1775, March 18, 1 Sm.L. 422, § 4.

21 P. S. § 45. Proof of deeds without subscribing witnesses, where one or more of the parties is dead

Where there is no subscribing witness to any deed and conveyance, or other instrument of writing, concerning lands, tenements or hereditaments, which might be recorded if probated according to existing laws, and any of the parties thereto shall be deceased, it shall and may be lawful to and for any of the judges of the supreme court, or any judge, learned in the law, of the court of common pleas of the county where the lands lie, to take the examination of any witness or witnesses, on oath or affirmation, to prove the handwriting of such deceased party or parties, and of the surviving party or parties which shall be certified by the judge before whom such proof shall be made; and such deed, conveyance or other instrument of writing, being so proved by two or more witnesses, and so certified, shall be recorded as in other cases under the acts relating to the recording of deeds: Provided, That in addition to the proofs so made by two or more witnesses the surviving party or parties to such deed, conveyance or other instrument of writing, shall also be examined, on oath or affirmation, before said judge, as to the handwriting of such deceased party.

1878, May 25, P.L. 155, § 1.

21 P. S. § 46. Certificate of acknowledgment prima facie evidence thereof and of execution

Where any deed, conveyance or other instrument of writing has been or shall be made and executed, either within or out of this state, and the acknowledgment or proof thereof duly certified, by any officer under seal, according to the existing laws of this commonwealth, for the purpose of being recorded therein, such certificate shall be deemed prima facie evidence of such execution and acknowledgment, or proof, without requiring proof of the said seal, as fully, to all intents and purposes, and with the same effect only, as if the same had been so acknowledged or proved before any judge, justice of the peace or alderman within this commonwealth.

1840, April 3, P.L. 233, § 1.

The form of certificate of acknowledgment of individuals (single or married) of any deed may be in the following words:

Commonwealth of Pennsylvania, }
                                          } ss:
County of _____ }
On this _____ day of _____ A. D. 19__, before me, a _____ in and for _____, came the above named _____ and acknowledged the foregoing deed to be _____ act and deed, and desired the same to be recorded as such.

Witness my hand and _____ seal, the day and year aforesaid.

(Seal)

_____

_____

(Official character.) My commission expires _____

1909, April 1, P.L. 91, § 8; 1925, April 30, P.L. 404, § 8.

21 P. S. § 82. Acknowledgments by married woman

Acknowledgments of any married woman of any deeds, mortgages or other instruments of writing, required by law to be acknowledged, shall be taken by any judge, justice of the peace, notary public, or other person authorized by law to take acknowledgments of deeds, et cetera, in same manner and form as though said married woman were feme-sole; said acknowledgment to have the same force and effect as if taken separate and apart from the husband of said married woman.

1901, April 4, P.L. 67, § 1.

EXECUTION OR ACKNOWLEDGMENT BY CORPORATIONS

21 P. S. § 111. Corporate acknowledgments by appointed attorney; form of appointment

A corporation may acknowledge any deed, conveyance, mortgage or other instrument of writing by an attorney appointed by such corporation, and such appointment may be embodied in said deed, conveyance, mortgage or other instrument of writing in substantially the following form: The (name of corporation) doth hereby constitute and appoint (name of appointee) to be its attorney for it, and in its name and as and for its corporate act and deed to acknowledge this (name of instrument), before any person having authority by the laws of the commonwealth of Pennsylvania to take such acknowledgment, to the intent that the same may be duly recorded.

1901, May 11, P.L. 171, § 1.

21 P. S. § 112. Who may take such acknowledgment; form of certificate

Such acknowledgment may be made before any person or officer now or hereafter to be authorized by the laws of this commonwealth to take acknowledgments of deeds or other instruments of writing, whose certificate of such acknowledgment shall be in substantially the following form:

I hereby certify that on this _____ day of _____, in the year of our Lord and _____, before me, the subscriber (title of officer taking acknowledgment), personally appeared (name of attorney) the attorney named in the foregoing (name of instrument), and by virtue and in pursuance of the authority therein conferred upon him, acknowledged the said (name of instrument) to be the act of the said (corporation's name). Witness my hand and _____ seal the day and year aforesaid.

1901, May. 11, P.L. 171, § 2.

REGISTRATION AND RECORDING
UNIFORM REAL PROPERTY ELECTRONIC RECORDING ACT

21 P. S. § 483.3. Validity of electronic documents.

(a) Requirement for original.--If a law requires, as a condition for recording, that a document be an original, either on paper or another tangible medium, or be in writing, the requirement is satisfied by an electronic document that complies with the provisions of this act.

(b) Signature.--If a law requires, as a condition for recording, that a document be signed, the requirement is satisfied by an electronic signature.

(c) Notarization.--The following shall apply:

(1) A requirement that a document or a signature associated with a document be notarized, acknowledged, verified, witnessed or made under oath is satisfied if:

(i) The electronic signature of the person authorized to perform that act, and all other information required to be included, is attached to or logically associated with the document or signature.

(ii) The act comports with the requirements of Chapters 1, 3 and 5 of the act of December 16, 1999 (P.L.971, No.69), known as the Electronic Transactions Act.

(iii) With respect to notarizations, the act comports with the requirements and procedures of the act of August 21, 1953 (P.L.1323, No.373), known as The Notary Public Law, pertaining to electronic notarization, acknowledgment and verification.

(2) A physical or electronic image of a stamp, impression or seal need not accompany an electronic signature.

(d) Record retention.--This act does not preclude the Pennsylvania Historical and Museum Commission from specifying additional requirements for retention of a record subject to the commission's jurisdiction, including the requirement that the recorder retain a record in a nonelectronic form.

TITLE 73. TRADE AND COMMERCE
CHAPTER 41. REGULATORY ELECTRONIC TRANSACTIONS

CHAPTER 3. UNIFORM ELECTRONIC TRANSACTIONS

73 P. S. § 2260.307. Notarization and acknowledgment

If a law requires a signature or record to be notarized, acknowledged, verified or made under oath, the requirement is satisfied if the electronic signature of the person authorized to perform those services, together with all other information required to be included by other applicable law, is attached to or logically associated with the signature or record.

1999, Dec. 16, P.L. 971, No. 69, § 307, effective in 30 days.

CHAPTER 51. MISCELLANEOUS PROVISIONS

73 P. S. § 2260.5101. Effective date

This act shall take effect as follows:

(1) Section 307 shall take effect 30 days following the publication in the Pennsylvania Bulletin of a notice by the Secretary of the Commonwealth that the provisions of section 307 no longer conflict with the requirements and procedures of the act of August 21, 1953 (P.L. 1323, No. 373), known as The Notary Public Law, or its successor with regard to electronic notarization, acknowledgment and verification.

(2) This section shall take effect immediately.

(3) The remainder of this act shall take effect in 30 days.

1999, Dec. 16, P.L. 971, No. 69, § 5101, effective in 30 days.

PENNSYLVANIA CODE
PROPOSED, NOT YET ENACTED
TITLE 4
ADMINISTRATION
* * *

PART VIII. BUREAU OF COMMISSIONS, ELECTIONS AND LEGISLATION
SUBPART C. COMMISSIONS AND NOTARIES PUBLIC

Chapter 161. Fees

§ 161.2. Notary public fee schedule

(a) The fees of notaries public as fixed by the Department of State pursuant to section 329.1 of the Revised Uniform Law on Notarial Acts (Act 73 of 2013) (57 Pa.C.S. §329.1) are:

Taking acknowledgment	$ 5
Taking acknowledgments (each additional name)	$ 2
Administering oath or affirmation (per individual taking oath or affirmation)	$ 5

Taking verification on oath or affirmation
(no matter how many signatures).. $ 5
Witnessing or attesting a signature (per signature)........................... $ 5
Certifying or attesting a copy or deposition
(per certified copy)... $ 5
Noting a protest of a negotiable instrument (per page) .... $ 3

(b) A notary public may charge a clerical or administrative fee for services related to a notarial act, such as copying, postage, travel and telephone calls. If charging clerical or administrative fees, the notary must inform the customer of the amount of each fee prior to performing the service. Clerical or administrative fees must be reasonable.

(c) A notary public shall provide an itemized receipt for all fees charged by the notary public.

(d) A notary public may not charge any fee under subsection (a) for notarizing the supporting affidavit required in an Emergency Absentee Ballot or the affidavit of a person needing assistance to vote an absentee ballot.

(e) A notary public may not charge a fee under subsection (a) where other applicable law dictates that no fee may be charged. Cross reference 51 Pa.C.S. § 9101 (Acknowledgments and administering oaths without charge).

(f) A notary public shall display or provide fees in accordance with section 329.1(c)(3). For purposes of display of fees, a place of business is the notary's business office, residence or any other location where the notary public performs a notarial act.

Chapter 165. [Notaries Public] [Reserved].

[§ 165.1. Lesser offenses incompatible with the duties of a notary public— statement of policy.

(a) The Secretary of the Commonwealth reviews applications for appointment to the office of notary public under section 5 of The Notary Public Law (act) (57 P. S. § 151). Section 5(b)(1) of the act requires that the applicant may not have been convicted of or pled guilty or nolo contendere to a felony or a lesser offense incompatible with the duties of a notary public during the 5-year period preceding the date of the application.

(b) Misdemeanor crimes involving a lack of honesty or elements of falsehood and fraud (crimen falsi) are considered incompatible with the duties of a notary public, regardless of the jurisdiction in which crimes were committed.

(c) Under Pennsylvania law, misdemeanors include, but are not limited to, the following:

(1) Forgery and fraudulent practices which includes bad checks, insurance fraud and identity theft. See 18 Pa.C.S. Chapter 41 (relating to forgery and fraudulent practices).

(2) Theft which includes receiving stolen property and retail theft. See 18 Pa.C.S. Chapter 39 (relating to theft and related offenses).

(3) Criminal conspiracy if the underlying crime is incompatible. See 18 Pa.C.S. § 903 (relating to criminal conspiracy).

(4) Bribery. See 18 Pa.C.S. § 4701 (relating to bribery in official and political matters).

(5) Perjury or falsification in official matter which includes false swearing, unsworn falsification to authorities and tampering with evidence. See 18 Pa.C.S. Chapter 49, Subchapter A (relating to perjury and falsification in official matters).

(6) Obstructing governmental operations. See 18 Pa.C.S. Chapter 51, Subchapter A (relating to definition of offenses generally).

(d) The Secretary will consider all similar crimes committed in the courts of the United States or any other state, territory, possession or country to be incompatible with the duties of a notary public.]

Chapter 167. Notaries Public

Subchapters
A. General Provisions
B. Qualifications for appointment and commission
C. Official Stamp, Stamping Device and Embosser
D. Notary Journal
E. Standards of Practice
F. Notarial Acts
G. Notarial Certificates
H. Use of Electronic Notarization
I. Notary Public Education
J. Examination
K. Prohibited Acts and Sanctions

Subchapter A. General Provisions

§ 167.1. Scope
The rules in this chapter implement Chapter 3 of Title 57 of the Pennsylvania Consolidated Statutes (the Revised Uniform Law on Notarial Acts). The rules govern the qualification, commissioning, notarial acts, conduct and discipline of notaries public in the Commonwealth of Pennsylvania.

§ 167. 2. Definitions
The following words and terms, when used in this chapter, have the following meanings, unless the context clearly indicates otherwise:

Act – the Revised Uniform Law on Notarial Acts (57 Pa. C.S. §§ 301—331).

Address – Includes office address and home address. A post office box number is not a sufficient address for Department of State records.

Applicant – an individual who seeks appointment or reappointment to the office of notary public

Appoint or Appointment – the naming of an individual to the office of notary public after determination that the individual has complied with 57 Pa.C.S. § 321(a) and (b) of the Revised Uniform Law on Notarial Acts and Subchapter B (relating to Qualifications for appointment and commission) of this Chapter. Also includes the terms "reappoint" and "reappointment."

Appointee – an individual who has been appointed or reappointed to the office of notary public bbut has not yet taken the oath of office to be commissioned.

Bureau – Bureau of Commissions, Elections and Legislation of the Pennsylvania Department of State.

Days – Means calendar days.

Department – The Department of State of the Commonwealth of Pennsylvania.

Examination – The examination described in § 167.111.

Journal – The term includes a notary register.

Notary – As used in this chapter, means notary public.

Official stamp or Official Notary Stamp – The term includes a notary seal image. An official stamp does not include a stamping device as defined in 57 Pa.C.S. §302 or an embosser.

Spouse – An individual holding a marriage license issued or recognized under Chapter 13 of the Domestic Relations Code who is married to a notary public.

Tangible – When used in conjunction with "record," "medium" or "symbol," means perceptible by touch

Subchapter B. Qualifications for Appointment and Commission

§ 167.11. Eligibility for appointment and commission – applicants not residing in Pennsylvania

(a) If an applicant is not a resident of Pennsylvania, the applicant must have a place of employment or practice in this Commonwealth.

(b) Employment or practice in this Commonwealth shall be on an ongoing basis.

(c) The Bureau may request that employment or practice in this Commonwealth be evidenced by written confirmation from the employer that a notary commission is required for such employment or practice.

§ 167.12. Eligibility for appointment and commission – applicants holding state and federal office

The disqualifications of 65 P.S. § 1 (relating to State and federal offices) apply to individuals who are elected or appointed to any office under the legislative, executive or judiciary departments of the United States government. Individuals who are employed by the legislative, executive or judiciary departments of the United States government, but who are neither elected nor appointed to office, are eligible for appointment and commission as a notary public.

§ 167.13. Eligibility for appointment and commission – deemed resignation

If a notary public neither resides nor works in the Commonwealth, that notary public shall be deemed to have resigned from the office of notary public as of the date the residency ceases or employment within the Commonwealth terminates. A notary public who resigns that notary's commission in accordance with this section shall notify the Department of State in writing or electronically within 30 days of the effective date of the resignation.

§ 167.14. Application for appointment

(a) First-time applicants. At the same time the application for appointment is submitted, the applicant shall submit evidence of passing the examination and successful completion of a basic education course.

(b) Reappointments. At the same time the application for appointment is submitted, the applicant shall submit evidence of successful completion of a basic education or continuing education course.

(c) Applications for appointment shall be typed or legibly written.

(d) The applicant's signature on the application must match the applicant's name as provided on the application. The applicant shall use a legible, recognizable handwritten signature, which can be attributed to the applicant by anyone examining or authenticating the signature. If an applicant's preferred signature is not legible and recognizable, the applicant must also legibly print his or her name immediately adjacent to his or her preferred signature. For the purposes of this subsection, a signature is legible and recognizable if it is distinct, easily readable and understandable, and the notary's full name may be clearly discerned by looking at the signature.

§ 167.15. Appointment and issuance of commission

(a) Upon determination that an applicant has complied with all requirements of the Act and this Chapter, the Department shall appoint or reappoint the applicant to the office of notary public and issue a commission certificate.

(b) The Department shall send the commission certificate to the Recorder of Deeds of the
county where the notary maintains an office.

(c) The Department shall send the appointee notice that:

(1) The commission certificate has been issued and sent to the proper Recorder of Deeds;

(2) The appointee shall obtain a bond without delay;

(3) The appointee shall appear within 45 days of the date of appointment to take the oath of office before the Recorder of Deeds in the proper county and record the bond, oath and commission in the office of the Recorder of Deeds; and

(4) The appointee shall register his or her official signature in the proper county and office within 45 days of the date of appointment pursuant to section 321(d.1) of the Act.

(d) Before taking the oath of office or registering an official signature, an appointee shall present satisfactory evidence of the appointee's identity as set out in section 307(b) of the Act and these regulations.

(e) After administering the oath of office, the Recorder of Deeds shall deliver the commission certificate to the notary public.

§ 167.16. Reappointment if Bond, Oath and Commission not

Recorded Within 45 Days

(a) The commission of a notary public who fails to record the bond, oath and commission or register his or her official signature within 45 days of appointment shall be null and void.

(b) An appointee who fails to record the bond, oath and commission within 45 days of appointment may reapply for reappointment.

(c) The appointee shall:

(1) Reapply for reappointment;

(2) Submit another application fee;

(3) Submit evidence of passing the examination, if a first-time applicant; and

(4) Submit evidence of completion of basic or continuing education.

(d) All certificates for examination and education shall be valid at the time of application for reappointment.

§ 167.17. Reappointment

Applications for reappointment to the office of notary public shall be filed at least 60 days prior to the expiration of the commission under which the notary is acting.

§ 167.18. Notification of Change in Information

(a) A notary public must notify the Department of State within 30 days of any change in the information on file with the Department, including the notary's:

(1) Legal Name

(2) Office address (includes place of employment or practice in Pennsylvania, if not a resident of the Commonwealth)

(3) Home address

(4) Name of electronic notarization vendor

(5) Voluntary resignation

(b) Such notice may be made in writing or electronically and shall state the effective date of such change.

(c) Notice of a change in legal name on file with the Department shall be on a form prescribed by the Department and accompanied by evidence of the name change (such as marriage certificate, court order, divorce decree).

(d) Notice of a change in legal name on file with the Department shall also be made to the recorder of deeds of the county in which the notary public maintains an office.

§ 167.19. Change of name

(a) When the legal name of a notary is changed, the notary may continue to perform official acts, in the name in which he or she was commissioned, until the expiration of his or her term.

(b) The Department shall mark the public records relating to the notary name change. Application for reappointment of such notary shall be made in the new name.

Subchapter C. Official Stamp, Stamping Device and Embosser

§ 167.21. Official stamp

(a) The official stamp of a notary public must show clearly in the following order:

(1) The words "Commonwealth of Pennsylvania – Notary Seal."

(2) The name as it appears on the commission of the notary and the words "Notary Public."

(3) The name of the county in which the notary public maintains an office.

(4) The date the notary's current commission expires.

(5) The seven-digit commission identification number assigned by the Department.

(b) No words or terms on the official stamp may be abbreviated.

(c) The official stamp or notary seal shall be stamped or affixed to the notarial certificate near the notary's signature or attached to or logically associated with an electronic record containing the notary's signature.

(d) A notary public shall not place an imprint of the notary's official stamp over any signature in a record to be notarized or over any writing in a notarial certificate.

(e) A notary public shall not alter or deface the official stamp.

(f) A notary public shall not use the notary public's official stamp for any purpose other than to perform a notarial act.

(g) A notary public shall not permit any other person to use the notary public's official stamp for any purpose.

(h) A notary public shall not use any other notary public's official stamp or any other object in lieu of the notary's own official stamp to perform a notarial act.

(i) Transitional provision. A notary public who holds a commission on the effective date of this section may continue to use his seal until the expiration of that commission, which may occur after the effective date of this section.

Example of stamp:

```
Commonwealth of Pennsylvania – Notary Seal
John Q. Doe, Notary Public
Dauphin County
My commission expires May 19, 2021
Commission number 1234567
```

§ 167.22. Stamping device

(a) A stamping device, as used in section 302 and section 318 of Title 57 of the Pennsylvania Consolidated Statutes, does not include a non-inking embosser or crimper.

(b) A stamping device must be capable of affixing or logically associating the official stamp, such that the record to which the official stamp is so affixed or associated may be copied, filmed, scanned, or otherwise legibly reproduced.

(c) The stamping device is the exclusive property of the notary public. When not in use, the stamping device shall be kept in a secure location and accessible only to the notary. A secure location includes in the notary's sole possession or in a locked location to which only the notary has access.

(d) Notification of loss or theft of stamping device under section 318(b) shall be made in writing or electronically to the Department within ten days after the date the notary public or personal representative or guardian discovers that the stamping device was lost, misplaced, stolen or is otherwise unavailable. The notification shall include:

(1) A statement of whether the stamping device is lost, misplaced, stolen or is otherwise unavailable;

(2) The date the notary public discovered that the official stamping device was lost, misplaced, stolen or is otherwise unavailable;

(3) A statement that the notary public does not possess the stamping device and does not know who possesses it or where it is located;

(4) A statement that if the notary public subsequently reacquires possession of the lost, misplaced, stolen or otherwise unavailable stamping device, then the notary public shall file a statement with the Department within ten days after the date the notary public reacquires possession of the lost, misplaced, stolen or otherwise unavailable stamping device;

(e) If a notary public subsequently reacquires possession of a lost, misplaced, or stolen stamping device, then the notary public shall file with the Department a written statement of explanation within ten days after the date the notary public reacquires possession of the lost, misplaced or stolen stamping device.

(f) An individual whose notary public commission has been suspended or revoked shall deliver the stamping device to the Department of State within ten days after notice of the suspension or revocation from the Department.

§ 167. 23. Embosser

(a) A notary public may use an embossed or crimped image in the performance of a notarial act, but only in conjunction with the use of an official stamp.

(b) A notary public shall not place the embossing or crimping over any signature or printed material in a record to be notarized, or over any signature or printed material in a notarial certificate.

(c) A notary public shall not use any other notary public's embosser or any other object in lieu of the notary public's official stamp to perform a notarial act.

Subchapter D. Notary Journal

§ 167.31. Identification of Notary in Journal

(a) Each journal of a notary public, whether maintained on a tangible medium or in an electronic format, shall contain the following information in any order:

(1) The name of the notary public as it appears on the commission;
(2) The notary public's commission number;
(3) The notary public's commission expiration date;
(4) The notary public's office address of record with the Department;
(5) A statement that, in the event of the decease of the notary public, the journal shall be delivered or mailed to the office of the recorder of deeds in the country where the notary last maintained an office;
(6) The meaning of any not commonly abbreviated word or symbol used in recording a notarial act in the notarial journal;
(7) The signature of the notary public;
(b) If a notary public's name, commission expiration date, or address changes before the notary public ceases to use the notarial journal, the notary public shall add the new information after the old information and the date which the information changed.

§ 167.32. Journal Entries.

(a) Each notarial act shall be indicated as a separate entry in the journal.

(b) Optional entries. In addition to the entries required by section 319(c) of the Act, a notary journal may contain the signature of the individual for whom the notarial act is performed and any additional information about a specific transaction which might assist the notary to recall the transaction.

(c) Prohibited entries. A notary journal may not contain any personal financial or identification information about the notary's clients, such as complete Social Security numbers, complete drivers' license numbers or complete account numbers. Terminal numbers for these types of numbers, including the last four digits of a Social Security number, may be used to clarify which individual or account was involved.

(d) Fees. Each notarial fee charged should correspond to the notarial act performed. If a fee is waived or not charged, the notary public shall indicate this fact in the journal entry, using "n/c" or "0" (zero) or a similar notation. Clerical and administrative fees, if charged, must be separately itemized in the journal.

(e) Address. For purpose of journal entries, address means the city and state only.

(f) For the purpose of subsection (c), "personal financial or identification information" means:

(1) An individual's first name or first initial and last name in combination with and linked to any one or more of the following data elements when the data elements are not encrypted or redacted:

(i) Social Security number.

(ii) Driver's license number or a State identification card number issued in lieu of a driver's license.

(iii) Financial account number, credit or debit card number, in combination with any required security code, access code or password that would permit access to an individual's financial account.

(2) The term does not include publicly available information that is lawfully made available to the general public from Federal, State or local government records.

(g) Transitional provision. A notary public who holds a commission on the effective date of this section may continue to use his journal until the expiration of that commission, which may occur after the effective date of this section.

§ 167.33. Form and Content of Notary Journal Maintained on a Tangible Medium

(a) A journal of a notary public maintained on paper or on any other tangible medium may be in any form that meets the physical requirements set out in this rule and the entry requirements set out in section 319(c) of the Act.

(b) The cover and pages inside the cover shall be bound together by any binding method that is designed to prevent the insertion, removal or substitution of the cover or a page. This includes glue, staples, grommets or another binding, but does not include the use of tape, paperclips or binder clips.

(c) Each page shall be consecutively numbered from the beginning to the end of the journal. If a journal provides two pages on which to record the required information about the same notarial act, then both pages may be numbered with the same number or each page may be numbered with a different number. A page number shall be preprinted.

(d) Each line (or entry if the journal is designed with numbered entry blocks) shall be consecutively numbered from the beginning to the end of the page. If a line extends across two pages, the line shall be numbered with the same number on both pages. A line or entry number shall be preprinted.

§ 167.34. Form and Content of an Electronic Notarial Journal

(a) A journal of a notary public maintained in electronic format may be in any form that meets the requirements set out in this rule and the entry requirements set out in section 319(c) of the Act.

(b) A journal of a notary public maintained in electronic format shall be designed to prevent the insertion, removal or substitution of an entry.

(c) A journal of a notary public maintained in electronic format shall be securely stored and recoverable in the event of a hardware or software malfunction.

(d) Entries from the notarial journal must be available upon demand by the Department in a PDF format.

(e) If a signature of a signer is contained in an electronic notarial journal, the signature must be:

(1) Attached to or logically associated with the electronic journal.

(2) Linked to the data in such a manner that any subsequent alterations to the electronic notarial journal entry are detectable and may invalidate the electronic notarial journal entry.

(f) A journal of a notary public maintained in electronic format which is delivered to the office of the recorder of deeds in compliance with section 319(e) of the Act shall be delivered in a format prescribed by the receiving recorder of deeds.

§ 167.35. Notification of Lost or Stolen Journal

(a) A notary shall maintain custody and control of the notary journal at all times during the duration of the notary's commission.

(b) Notification of loss or theft of journal under section 319(d) of the Act shall be made in writing or electronically within ten days after the date the notary public or personal representative or guardian discovers that the journal was lost, misplaced, destroyed or otherwise unavailable. The notification shall include:

(1) A statement of whether the notary journal is lost, misplaced, stolen or is otherwise unavailable;

(2) An explanation of how the notary journal became unavailable;

(3) The date the notary public discovered that the notary journal was lost, misplaced, stolen or is otherwise unavailable;

(3) A statement that the notary public does not possess the journal and does not know who possesses it or where it is located;

(4) A statement that if the notary public subsequently reacquires possession of the lost, misplaced, stolen or otherwise unavailable journal, then the notary public shall file a statement with the Department within ten days after the date the notary public reacquires possession of the lost, misplaced, or stolen journal;

(c) If a notary public subsequently reacquires possession of a lost, misplaced, or stolen journal, then the notary public shall file with the Department a written statement of explanation within ten days after the date the notary public reacquires possession of the lost, misplaced, stolen or otherwise unavailable journal.

§ 167.36. Certified copies of notary journal

(a) General. Requests for certified copies of a notary journal made in accordance with section 319(g.1) of the Act shall be reasonable in scope and specify the particular entry or time period sought. Such requests may, but are not required to be, in writing. The notary public shall provide the certified copy within 10 days of receipt of the request. The notary may charge reasonable fees for copying and postage, but the requestor should be advised in advance of these fees. If the scope of the request is not clear, the notary may offer to have the requester inspect the journal at the notary's office to identify the specific pages or dates that the requester is seeking.

(b) Subpoenas and investigative requests. A request for certified copies of a notary journal made through an investigative request by law enforcement or by the Department or in a subpoena in the course of criminal or civil litigation shall be complied with in the manner specified in the request or subpoena.

Subchapter E. Standards of Practice

§ 167. 41. Name of notary public

(a) Whenever chapter 3 of Title 57 of the Pennsylvania Consolidated Statutes and Chapter 167 of this Title refer to the name of a notary public, the name shall be the legal name of the notary public as it appears on the notary public's current commission and oath of office.

(b) For the purposes of this chapter, the legal name on the notary public commission and oath of office must be proven by satisfactory evidence per §307(b) of Title 57 of the Pennsylvania Consolidated Statutes. Unless proven otherwise, the name of a notary public shall consist of:

(i) a first personal name (first name), additional name(s) or initial(s) (middle name or initial), and surname (family or last name);

(ii) a first name and last name, omitting the middle name or middle initial;

(iii) a first initial, middle name and last name.

Neither initials alone nor nicknames will be accepted on the application or as part of the signature required on a notarial act.

(c) The name of a notary public may include suffixes such as Junior, Senior, II, III, IV or any abbreviations thereof. The name of a notary public may not include prefixes, suffixes or titles such as "Doctor," "Reverend" or "Esquire" or any abbreviations thereof.

§ 167.42. Authority of notary public to perform notarial act

(a) A notary may perform the notarial acts authorized by chapter 3 of Title 57 in any county of this Commonwealth.

(b) Notaries may not perform the notarial acts authorized by chapter 3 of Title 57 outside the geographical borders of this Commonwealth or in other states or jurisdictions, unless authorized by the other state or jurisdiction to perform such acts.

§ 167.43. Conflict of interest

(a) A direct or pecuniary interest includes an interest in the transaction or record which results in actual or potential gain or advantage, financial or otherwise, other than receiving a regular salary, hourly wage or notarial fees. Regular salary or wage includes bonuses, as long as such bonus is not related to or contingent upon the completion of a notarial act.

(b) In the case of a nomination petition or nomination paper, both the candidate and the spouse of the candidate have a direct or pecuniary interest in the nomination petition or nomination paper. No other person, including other family members, staff or other employees of the candidate or the candidate's spouse, or of the candidate's campaign or official office, shall be deemed to have a direct or pecuniary interest in the nomination petition or nomination paper.

(c) A notary shall not notarize his or her own signature, nor the signature of his or her spouse.

§ 167.44. Duty of candor

A notary public or an applicant for appointment and commission as a notary has a duty of candor to the Department in all matters relating to the appointment and commission of the notary and the performance of notarial acts, including an application for appointment or reappointment, and any request for information made by the Department.

§ 167.45. Personal appearance

(a) To appear personally before a notarial officer is to be physically present before the notarial officer when the notarial act is executed.

(b) The notarial officer must be able to observe and interact with the individual making the statement or executing the signature.

(c) The notarial officer and the individual for whom a notarial act is being performed must be able to see, hear, communicate with, and give identification documents to each other without the use of electronic devices such as telephones, computers, video cameras, or facsimile machines.

(d) Personal appearance does not include:

(1) Appearance by video technology, even if the video is live or synchronous;

(2) Appearance by audio technology.

§ 167.46. Identification of individual appearing before notarial officer – Personal knowledge

When a notarial officer has personal knowledge of the identity of an individual, satisfactory evidence is not required.

§ 167.47. Identification of individual appearing before notarial officer – Satisfactory evidence

(a) General

(1) For the purposes of section 307(b)(1)(i), a notarial officer may rely upon:

(i) A passport or passport card issued by the United States Department of State which is current and unexpired;

(ii) A passport issued by a foreign government, which is current and unexpired, provided it uses letters, characters and a language that are read, written and understood by the notarial officer;

(iii) A driver's license or nondriver identification card issued by a state of the United States, which is current and unexpired; or

(iv) A driver's license or nondriver identification card issued by a state or territory of Canada or Mexico, which is current and unexpired, provided it uses letters, characters and a language that are read, written and understood by the notarial officer.

(2) For the purposes of 307(b)(1)(ii), other forms of government identification must be current, contain the signature or photograph of the individual to be identified and must be satisfactory to the notarial officer. Current means having an issue date which is prior to the notarial act.

(3) For the purposes of section 307(b)(1)(ii), other forms of government identification may include:

(i) Identification card issued by any branch of the U.S. armed forces

(ii) An inmate identification card issued by the Pennsylvania Department of Corrections for an inmate who is currently in the custody of the Department

(iii) An identification card issued by the U.S. Department of Homeland Security

(iv) Social Security card

(v) Medicare card

(vi) Pennsylvania state and state-related university identification card

(b) Credible Witness.

(1) The identity of the individual appearing before the notarial officer can be established by the oath of a single credible witness personally known to the notary and who personally knows the document signer.

(2) A credible witness may not have a direct or pecuniary interest with respect to the record being notarized.

(3) The credible witness must make a verification on oath or affirmation that each of the following is true:

(i) The individual appearing before the notary public as the signer of the document is the person named in the document;

(ii) The credible witness personally knows the signer;

(iii) The credible witness reasonably believes that the circumstances of the signer are such that it would be very difficult or impossible for the signer to obtain another form of identification;

(iv) The signer does not possess any of the identification documents authorized by law to establish the signer's identity; and

(v) The credible witness does not have a direct or pecuniary interest in the record being notarized.

§ 167.48. Language and use of interpreter

(a) A notarial officer must be able to communicate directly with the individual for whom a notarial act is being performed in a language they both understand or indirectly through an interpreter who is physically present with the signer and notary at the time of the notarization and communicates directly with the individual and the notary in a language the interpreter understands.

(b) The certificate of notarial act must be worded and completed using only letters, characters and a language that are read, written and understood by the notarial officer.

(c) A notarial officer may perform a notarial act on a document that is a translation of a document that is in a language that the notarial officer does not understand only if the person performing the translation signs a verification on oath or affirmation stating that the translation is accurate and complete. The notarized translation and verification shall be attached to the document and shall comply with the Act and these regulations relating to certificate of notarial act.

§ 167.49. Refusal to perform notarial acts

A notary public may not refuse to provide notarial services on the basis of a customer's race, color, national origin, religion, sexual orientation, gender identity (including pregnancy), disability or marital status.

§ 167.50. Notarizing documents which contain blank spaces

(a) A notary public may not perform a notarial act with respect to a record which is designed to provide information within blank spaces, where:

(1) The missing information has not been entered into a blank space; or

(2) The signature of an individual signing the record is not present, unless the individual is signing in the presence of the notary.

(b) For the purpose of subsection (a)(1), the missing information does not include:

(1) Any empty space with N/A or a line drawn through it; or

(2) Any additional signature lines designated for additional signers, if it is clear that the notarial act does not apply to the blank signature lines.

(c) A notarial officer performing a notarial act on nomination petitions or nomination papers with remaining empty lines for signatures should mark a line through those blank spaces for signatures, or an "X" across the blank signatures, to prevent the later addition of signatures after the notarization.

§ 167.51. Employer-employee relationship

Notwithstanding that an individual who holds a notary commission is responsible for exercising the duties and responsibilities of the notary commission, an employer, pursuant to an agreement with an employee who is or seeks to become a notary public, may pay for the education, testing, application or bond and the cost of any stamps, seals, or other supplies required in connection with the appointment, commission, or performance of the duties of such notary public. Such agreement may also provide for the remission of fees collected by such notary public to the employer, for the increased compensation of the notary public for the amount of notary fees collected and for reimbursement of the costs of obtaining a commission should the employee or employer terminate the employment.

§ 167.52. Limitation on provision of notarial services

Notwithstanding any other provision of law, an employer of a notary public may limit, during the employee's ordinary course of employment, the providing of notarial services by the employee solely to transactions directly associated with the business purposes of the employer.

Subchapter F. Notarial Acts

§ 167.61. Acknowledgments

(a) The individual making the acknowledgment shall appear personally before the notarial officer.

(b) The notarial officer shall have personal knowledge or satisfactory evidence of the identity of the individual making the acknowledgment.

(c) A record may be signed in the notarial officer's presence or a record may be signed prior to the acknowledgment. A record may not be signed subsequent to an acknowledgment.

(d) If the record is signed prior to appearance before the notarial officer, the individual making the acknowledgment shall acknowledge that the signature on the record is his or her own voluntary act.

(e) The notarial officer shall compare the signature on the record to the signature of the individual on the identification presented.

§ 167.62. Oaths and affirmations

(a) The individual taking the oath or affirmation shall appear personally before the notarial officer.

(b) The notarial officer shall have personal knowledge or satisfactory evidence of the identity of the individual taking the oath or affirmation.

(c) An oath or affirmation may be verbal or in writing. If in writing, the oath or affirmation shall be signed in the presence of the notarial officer.

(d) In administering an oath or affirmation, the notarial officer shall require the individual taking the oath to voluntarily swear or affirm that the statements contained in the oath are true or that the individual will perform an act or duty faithfully and truthfully.

§ 167.63. Verifications on oath or affirmation

(a) The individual making the verification on oath or affirmation shall appear personally before the notarial officer.

(b) The notarial officer shall have personal knowledge or satisfactory evidence of the identity of the individual making the verification on oath or affirmation.

(c) A record containing a statement which is being verified on oath or affirmation must be signed in the notarial officer's presence. A record containing a statement which is being verified may not be signed subsequent to the verification on oath or affirmation.

(d) The notarial officer shall compare the signature on the statement verified to the signature of the individual on the identification presented.

(e) In taking a verification on oath or affirmation, the notarial officer shall administer an oath to the individual making the statement and require that the individual voluntarily swear or affirm that the statements contained in the record are true.

§ 167.64. Witnessing or attestation of signatures

(a) The individual signing the record shall appear personally before the notarial officer.

(b) The notarial officer shall have personal knowledge or satisfactory evidence of the identity of the individual signing the record.

(c) A record containing a signature which is being witnessed or attested must be signed in the notarial officer's presence. A record containing a signature which is being witnessed or attested may not be signed subsequent to the witnessing or attestation of the signature.

(d) The notarial officer shall compare the signature on the record signed to the signature of the individual on the identification presented.

(e) The notarial act of witnessing or attesting a signature differs from an acknowledgment in that the party relying on the record may know for certain that the record was signed on the same date that the notarial officer affixed the official seal and signature to the document.

(f) The act of witnessing a signature differs from a verification on oath or affirmation in that the signer is merely signing the record, not swearing or affirming that the contents of the record are true.

§ 167.65. Certified or attested copies and depositions

(a) The notarial officer must be presented with the record, which may be in the possession of the requestor, or in the case where there is an official repository of records, in the care and possession of the notarial officer who may be the custodian of the official archive or collection.

(b) For paper records, the notarial officer shall compare the original document to a photocopy made by the requestor or by the notarial officer to determine that the photocopy or duplicate is a complete and accurate transcription or reproduction of the original record.

(c) For electronic records, the notarial officer shall compare the original record to a copy made by the requestor or by the notarial officer to determine that the copy is a complete and accurate transcription or reproduction of the original record.

(d) The notarial officer shall examine the record for alteration or tampering and to ensure that the original record itself is not a photocopy or copy.

(e) In issuing a certified or attested copy, the notary public does not guarantee the authenticity of the original document, its contents or its effects.

(f) Records for which a notary may not issue a certified copy include:

(1) Vital Records (birth and death certificates).

(2) U.S. Naturalization Certificates

(3) Any government-issued record which on its face states "do not copy," "illegal to copy" or words of similar meaning

(4) Any record which is prohibited by law to copy or certify

(g) Subject to subsections (f)(4) and (h), records for which a notary may issue a certified copy include:

(1) Public records

(2) Passports

(3) Drivers' licenses

(4) Transcripts

(5) Diplomas

(6) Contracts

(7) Leases

(8) Bills of sale

(9) Medical records, consents or waivers

(10) Powers of attorney

(h) For purpose of this section, a public record is defined as any record that is filed in or issued by a domestic or international federal, state or local government agency. If the record is intended to be sent overseas and will require an apostille or certification from the U.S. Department of State or Pennsylvania Department of State, the record must be certified by the office where the original or official copy of the record is maintained or by the public official who issued the record. Examples include deeds, marriage records, court orders and corporate documents filed with a state office or state repository as the official record.

§ 167.66. Protests of negotiable instrument

(a) A protest is a certificate of dishonor made by a United States consul or vice consul, or a notary public or other person authorized to administer oaths by the law of the place where dishonor occurs. It may be made upon information satisfactory to that person. The protest must:

(1) Identify the negotiable instrument;

(2) Certify either that presentment has been made or, if not made, the reason why it was not made, and

(3) State that the instrument has been dishonored by nonacceptance or nonpayment.

(b) The protest may also certify that notice of dishonor has been given to some or all parties.

(c) The individual requesting the protest shall appear personally before the notarial officer and be identified in the protest as the holder of the dishonored negotiable instrument.

(d) The notarial officer shall have personal knowledge or satisfactory evidence of the identity of the individual requesting the protest.

Subchapter G. Notarial Certificates

§ 167.71. Certificate of notarial act

(a) "Commonwealth of Pennsylvania" may be used in lieu of "State of Pennsylvania" on certificates of notarial acts.

(b) Sufficiency of certificate – A certificate must contain the information required by section 315(c) of the Act. A certificate may contain such other information as may be required to satisfy any legal requirements, or to satisfy ethical or legal concerns, or the business needs of the parties to the transaction.

(c) Securely attached – For purposes of attaching a notarial certificate to a tangible record, securely attached means stapled, grommetted or otherwise bound to the tangible record. Securely attached does not include the use of tape, paperclips or binder clips.

(d) When signing a paper certificate, the notary public shall use a legible, recognizable handwritten signature, which can be attributed to the notary performing the notarial act by anyone examining or authenticating the signature. If a notary's preferred signature is not legible and recognizable, the notary must also legibly print his or her name immediately adjacent to his or her preferred signature. For the purposes of this subsection, a signature is legible and recognizable if it is distinct, easily readable and understandable, and the notary's full name may be clearly discerned by looking at the signature.

Subchapter H. Use of Electronic Notarization

§ 167.81. Notification regarding use of electronic notarization

(a) A notary public who wishes to perform notarial acts with respect to electronic records must hold a current and unrestricted commission.

(b) A notary public who wishes to perform notarial acts with respect to electronic records shall be authorized by the Department to act as an "electronic notary" or "e-notary" prior to performing notarial acts with respect to electronic records.

(c) To obtain authorization, a notary public shall submit the following information to the Department in a manner prescribed by the Department:
(1) Name of notary public
(2) Commission number
(3) Office address
(4) Email address
(5) Name of electronic notarization solution provider
(6) Contact information for solution provider
(7) Website for solution provider

§ 167.82. Electronic notarization requirements

(a) A notary public performing notarial acts with respect to electronic records must use an electronic notarization solution approved by the Department. Before performing any electronic notarization, the notary shall take reasonable steps to ensure that the solution used is valid and has not expired, been revoked, or been terminated by the solution provider.

(b) All requirements of a notarial act performed with respect to a tangible record apply to an electronic record, including but not limited to, the personal appearance and identification of the individual appearing before the notary public, completion of a notarial certificate, use of an official stamp and recording of the notarial act in the notary journal.

Subchapter I. Notary Public Education

§ 167.91. Definitions

Certificate of Approval. A certificate issued by the Department under section 167.92 (relating to Provider certificate of approval) signifying that the provider named therein offers an education program curriculum preapproved by the Department of State and has complied with the requirements of these rules. The Certificate of Approval does not imply endorsement of any other products or services offered by the provider.

Certificate of Education. A certificate issued by a provider under section 167.97 (relating to Certificate of Education) signifying that the person named therein has successfully completed the approved education program provided by the provider.

Course of study. For the purposes of this subchapter, "course of study" applies to basic or continuing education, offered via live classroom instruction, correspondence course or interactive distance education means, such as online via the internet or other network technologies.

Notary public applicant. For the purposes of this subchapter, a "notary public applicant" is a person who must attend a course of instruction in order to qualify for commission as a notary public.

Pennsylvania business registration number. For the purposes of these rules, a Pennsylvania business registration number is the number assigned by the Department of State's Bureau of Corporations and Charitable Organizations to a business entity or fictitious name registrant that is authorized to conduct business in the Commonwealth.

Provider. For purposes of this subchapter, a "provider" is an individual or business entity that offers, supplies or provides an approved notary public education course of study.

§ 167.92. Provider Certificate of Approval

(a) Before offering any course of study pursuant to section 322(b) or (c), a provider must obtain a Certificate of Approval from the Department of State for each course of study offered.

(b) To apply for a Certificate of Approval, a provider must submit to the Department of State a completed Notary Public Education Provider Application or Amendment form on a form prescribed by the Department, an active Pennsylvania business registration number, the fee required by the Department and a lesson plan satisfying the requirements of section 167.93 (relating to Lesson Plan).

(c) The Department will issue either a Certificate of Approval, in accordance with subsection (d), or a deficiency notice, in accordance with section 167.94 (relating to Deficient application or lesson plan), within 90 days of receipt of an application and lesson plan.

(d) Upon approval of an application and lesson plan, the Department will send a Certificate of Approval to the provider by first class mail to the address listed on the Notary Public Education Provider Application or Amendment form.

(e) The Certificate of Approval will include the following:

(1) The name of the provider.

(2) The name of the approved course of study and whether it is basic education or continuing education.

(3) The date the course of study was approved by the Department.

(f) A provider must not alter or substitute the lesson plan reviewed and approved by the Department, unless the revisions are approved by the Department, in accordance with section 167.96 (relating to Lesson plan revisions).

(g) For the purposes of this chapter, a provider is responsible for all employees, agents, instructors, contractors, and subcontractors providing or involved in providing an approved course of study on behalf of the provider and the acts of the employees, agents, instructors, contractors, and subcontractors will be deemed the acts of the provider.

(h) The Certificate of Approval will expire three years from the date of issuance. A provider may reapply for reapproval of a notary public course of study up to 90 days before the expiration of the Certificate.

(i) A Certificate of Approval is non-transferable and may not be conveyed to another provider or applied to another course of study.

§ 167.93. Lesson Plan

(a) A lesson plan must meet the following requirements:

(1) The lesson plan must be based on the laws, regulations, procedures and ethics of Pennsylvania concerning the functions and duties of a notary public.

(2) The lesson plan must contain a table of contents, and the pages of the lesson plan must be consecutively numbered.

(3) The lesson plan must provide sufficient detail to enable the Department to evaluate the specific information to be presented and to determine the accuracy of the information to be presented.

(4) The lesson plan shall contain the procedures to establish the identity of a person physically attending a classroom course of study or virtually attending a course of study via interactive means to whom proof of completion may be issued in accordance with Section 167.97.

(5) The lesson plan shall contain the procedures to ensure that the information contained in the Certificate of Education pursuant to Section 167.97 cannot be viewed by any person other than the approved vendor issuing the certificate, an employee, agent, instructor, contractor, or subcontractor of the approved vendor issuing the certificate, or the notary public applicant or notary public named in the certificate.

(6) The lesson plan must contain the procedures to ensure that a person physically attending a classroom course of study or virtually attending a course of study via interactive means is present for the required time.

(7) The lesson plan must include a schedule of the time allotted for the following:

(a) Break periods, if any;

(b) Each major subject area;

(c) Each audio visual aid to be used, if any;

(d) Each student participation activity, if any.

(e) Completion, correction, and discussion of any practice tests used and the method of correction to be used, if any.

(8) If any movie or video is used for instruction, the lesson plan must include a brief synopsis of the information presented therein. The synopsis must detail the specific information presented by the movie or video. In addition, the provider must include the movie or video in the materials presented to the Department for review.

(b) Copies of any handout materials, workbooks, visuals aids, description of student participation exercises, and practice tests used during the course of study must be submitted for approval with the lesson plan.

(c) If the course provides for an evaluation by the students, time to complete the evaluation must not be included as part of the course of instruction.

(d) All materials submitted to the Department under this section become the property of the Department and may be returned to the provider at the sole discretion of the Department.

§ 167.94. Deficient Application or Lesson Plan

(a) If the Department of State determines that a Notary Public Education Provider Application or Amendment form is incomplete, or that a lesson plan does not satisfy the requirements of section 322 or this chapter, the Department will issue a deficiency notice containing an itemized description of the deficiencies identified. The deficiency notice will be sent by first class mail to the provider's address listed on the Notary Public Education Provider Application or Amendment form or communicated in a manner agreed to by the Department and the provider.

(b) A provider has 60 days from the date on which the deficiency notice was sent or communicated by the Department to submit documentation to the Department curing the deficiencies identified in the deficiency notice.

(c) The Department may issue more than one deficiency notice to a provider regarding the same Notary Public Education Provider Application or Amendment form and lesson plan at any time during the review process.

(d) The Department may disapprove a Notary Public Education Provider Application or Amendment form if the deficiencies are not cured in accordance with subsection (b).

(e) The disapproval of a provider's application or amendment is subject to the right of notice, hearing and adjudication and the right of appeal therefrom in accordance with 2 Pa.C.S. Chs. 5 Subch. A (relating to practice and procedure of Commonwealth agencies) and 7 Subch. A (relating to judicial review of Commonwealth agency action), known as the Administrative Agency Law.

§167.95. Notification of Changes of Provider Information

Within 30 days of any changes in the information contained in the most recent application approved by the Department, a provider must submit to the Department a Notary Public Education Provider Application or Amendment form identifying the changes. A provider may confirm receipt by the Department by phone or e-mail.

§ 167.96. Lesson Plan Revisions

(a) A provider shall revise an approved lesson plan as necessary to ensure that the information provided in an approved course of study reflects a new law, regulation, court decision or administrative action.

(b) Any proposed revisions to the contents or methods of instruction detailed in an approved lesson plan must be approved by the Department prior to implementing the proposed revisions in an approved course of study.

(c) To apply for a Certificate of Approval for a revised lesson plan, a provider must submit a completed Notary Public Education Provider Application or Amendment form, the fee required by the Department, and a revised lesson plan in accordance with Section 167.92 (relating to Provider certificate of approval).

(d) The provisions in Section 167.92 (Provider Certificate of Approval), Section 167.93 (Lesson Plan), and Section 167.94 (Deficient Application or Lesson Plan) apply to a revised lesson plan.

(e) Upon approval of a revised lesson plan, the Department of State will issue a Certificate of Approval pursuant to Section 167.92. (relating to Provider Certificate of Approval).

(f) A provider may only follow the lesson plan corresponding to the most current Certificate of Approval.

§ 167.97. Certificate of Education

(a) A provider must issue a Certificate of Education to a notary public applicant upon completion of an approved course of study.

(b) The Certificate of Education shall be issued by the provider to a notary public applicant only after the person has successfully completed the approved course of study.

(c) The Certificate of Education must consist of a certificate signed by a provider or an employee, agent, instructor, contractor, or subcontractor of a provider, which contains the following information:

(1) The name of the education provider as it appears on the Certificate of Approval issued by the Department of State for the approved course of study.

(2) The name of the approved course of study and whether it is basic education or continuing education.

(3) The name of the notary public applicant who completed the approved course of study.

(4) The date the notary public applicant completed the approved course of study.

(5) The statement that the Certificate of Education is valid for a period of six months from the date of issuance.

(d) A provider must submit all revisions to the contents or appearance of the Certificate of Education to the Department for approval at least 30 days prior to issuing the revised certificate to a notary public.

§ 167.98. List of Attendees

(a) A provider shall maintain a list of persons who attend each session of an approved course of study, whether they physically attend a classroom course of study or virtually attend a course of study offered via interactive means.

(b) The list of attendees must be maintained for a period of five years from the date of issuance of the Certificates of Education corresponding to that session.

(c) The list of attendees must include the following:

(1) The name of the provider as listed in the Certificate of Approval for the approved course of study.

(2) The name of the instructor or instructors who taught the approved course of study.

(3) The date, time, and location of the approved course of study.

(4) The names of all the attendees in alphabetical order by the last name of the attendee.

(c) A provider shall not collect the social security numbers of any attendees.

(d) Upon request, a provider shall submit a list of attendees in the data format specified by the Department of State.

§ 167.99. Department of State Attending Approved Course of Study

A provider must permit representatives of the Department of State to attend any approved course of study, without prior notice and at no charge, for the purpose of observation, monitoring, auditing, and investigating the instruction given.

§ 167.100. Duty to Respond to a Written Request from the Department of State

A provider must respond in writing within 30 days of receiving a written request for information from the Department of State. A written request may be sent to the mailing address, facsimile number, or e-mail address listed on the most current Notary Public Education Provider Application or Amendment form.

§ 167.101. Cancellation or Delay of Scheduled Approved Course of Study

(a) Before charging any fees to a notary public applicant for an approved course of study, a provider must disclose the refund policy of the provider.

(b) A provider must refund all fees within 30 days of a scheduled course date to any notary public applicant who registered to attend an approved course of study if one of the following occurs:

(1) An instructor fails to appear at the scheduled time, date, or place of the approved course of study;

(2) An approved course of study is delayed in starting more than 15 minutes after the scheduled time, and a notary public applicant immediately informs the provider of his or her request for a refund, and the notary public applicant leaves the approved course of study before its start; or

(3) The provider does not hold a current Certificate of Approval for the course of study.

§ 167.102. List of Approved Notary Education Courses

(a) The Department of State shall make a list of approved education courses available online at the Department's website. The approved course list will include the following information:

(1) Name of the approved course and whether it is approved for basic or continuing education.

(2) Name and contact information for the provider, including mailing address; telephone number; fax number; e-mail address; and website address.

(b) The Department shall update the list of approved courses to add, delete, or amend provider information that is filed in accordance with section 167.95 (relating to Notification of Changes of Education Provider Information) and add or delete courses that are approved or terminated in accordance with these rules.

§ 167.103. Termination of a Certificate of Approval

(a) The Department of State may terminate a Certificate of Approval upon any of the following grounds:

(1) Violation of any of the provisions of this chapter or the Revised Uniform Law on Notarial Acts.

(2) Misrepresentation of the laws of Pennsylvania concerning the duties and functions of a notary public.

(3) Deviation from the lesson plan for a course of study approved by the Department.

(4) Failure to respond to a request for information from the Department.

(5) Representations by the provider that any other product, goods, or services provided by the provider are endorsed or recommended by the Department.

(6) Failure to prepare course attendees to pass the notary public examination such that an adequate pass rate is not maintained

(b) Termination of a Certificate of Approval is subject to the right of notice, hearing and adjudication and the right of appeal therefrom in accordance with 2 Pa.C.S. Chs. 5 Subch. A (relating to practice and procedure of Commonwealth agencies) and 7 Subch. A (relating to judicial review of Commonwealth agency action), known as the Administrative Agency Law.

§ 167.104. Cancellation of Certificate of Approval

(a) A provider may cancel its Certificate of Approval by submitting a written notice of cancellation to the Department of State. Unless otherwise stated in the notice of cancellation, the effective date of the cancellation of the Certificate of Approval is 30 days after receipt of the notice of cancellation. The provider may confirm receipt by the Department by phone or e-mail.

(b) Within 30 days of the effective date of a cancellation of a Certificate of Approval, a provider must refund all fees to all individuals who paid to take an approved course from a provider, if the course is scheduled after the effective date of the cancellation.

Subchapter J. Examination

§ 167.111. Notary Public Examination.

(a) Pursuant to section 322(a) of the Revised Uniform Law on Notarial Acts (57 Pa.C.S. §322(a)), an applicant for a commission as a notary public who does not hold a commission in this Commonwealth must pass an examination as a condition of appointment. An applicant who does not hold a current commission as a notary public includes an applicant who never held a commission as a notary public and an applicant who previously held a commission as a notary public but whose commission has since expired.

(b) The written examination prescribed by the Department of State to determine the fitness of an applicant to exercise the functions of the office of notary public shall be a proctored examination administered by the Department of State or an agent of the Department. The examination is administered by a professional testing organization under contract with the Department at times, places and costs established by the professional testing organization.

(c) Examination results shall be valid for a period of one (1) year from the date of the examination.

(d) An applicant must score 80% or better to pass the examination.

(e) An applicant may retake the examination within a six-month period as many times as necessary to pass. The maximum frequency with which the examination may be repeated is one time per 24-hour period.

(f) More information about the examination is available through the Department's website at www.dos.pa.gov/OtherServices/Notaries.

Subchapter K. Prohibited Acts and Sanctions

§ 167.121. Offenses involving fraud, dishonesty or deceit.

(a) Conviction of, or acceptance of Accelerated Rehabilitative Disposition in resolution of, offenses involving a lack of honesty or elements of falsehood and fraud (crimen falsi) will be considered to be evidence of a lack of honesty, integrity, competence or reliability to act as a notary public, regardless of the jurisdiction in which the crimes were committed.

(b) Under Pennsylvania law, offenses involving fraud, dishonesty or deceit include, but are not limited to, the following:

(1) Theft and related offenses, which includes all offenses defined in subchapter B of 18 Pa.C.S. Chapter 39 (relating to theft and related offenses).

(2) Forgery and fraudulent practices, which includes all offenses defined in 18 Pa.C.S. Chapter 41 (relating to forgery and fraudulent practices).

(3) Bribery and related offenses, which includes all offenses defined in 18 Pa.C.S. Chapter 47 (relating to bribery and corrupt influence).

(4) Perjury or falsification in official matters and related offenses, which includes all offenses defined in Subchapter A of 18 Pa.C.S. Chapter 49 (relating to perjury and falsification in official matters).

(5) Obstructing governmental operations and related offenses, which includes all offenses defined in Subchapter A of 18 Pa.C.S. Chapter 51 (relating to definition of offenses generally).

(6) Abuse of office and related offenses, which includes all offenses defined in Chapter 53 of 18 Pa.C.S. (relating to abuse of office).

(7) Criminal attempt if the underlying crime involves fraud, dishonesty

or deceit. See 18 Pa.C.S. § 901 (relating to criminal attempt).

(8) Criminal solicitation if the underlying crime involves fraud, dishonesty or deceit. See 18 Pa.C.S. § 902 (relating to criminal solicitation).

(9) Criminal conspiracy if the underlying crime involves fraud, dishonesty or deceit. See 18 Pa.C.S. § 903 (relating to criminal conspiracy).

(c) The Department will consider all similar offenses committed in the courts of the United States, this Commonwealth or any other state, territory, possession or country involving fraud, dishonesty or deceit.

§ 167.122. Rebuttable presumption against appointment.

(a) Any person who has been convicted of or accepted Accelerated Rehabilitative Disposition for any felony offense or any misdemeanor offense involving fraud, dishonesty or deceit as set forth in § 167.121 within five (5) years preceding the date of application for appointment is presumed ineligible for appointment as a notary public.

(b) The presumption of ineligibility for appointment may be rebutted in extraordinary circumstances by a showing of clear and convincing evidence of the applicant's full rehabilitation. It is the intent of these regulations that overcoming this presumption will occur only infrequently and in truly exceptional circumstances.

(c) There is no presumption of ineligibility for conviction of or acceptance of ARD for a felony or an offense involving fraud, dishonesty or deceit more than five (5) years preceding the date of application for appointment, but the conviction and related facts may be considered in determining whether the applicant has the requisite honesty, integrity, competence or reliability to act as a notary public.

(d) The five-year period shall be measured from the date of the conviction or acceptance into ARD, rather than the date of the act(s) which constituted the offense(s).

(e) For the purposes of this subchapter, the terms "conviction" and "convicted of" shall include a conviction after a bench or jury trial, a guilty plea, a plea of nolo contendere or a finding of not guilty due to insanity or of guilty but mentally ill. Acceptance of Accelerated Rehabilitative Disposition ("ARD") is regardless of whether the court considers it a conviction or a form of judgment without verdict.

§ 167.123. Reporting of crimes, disciplinary action and other matters.

(a) A notary public shall notify the Department of conviction of or acceptance of accelerated rehabilitative disposition in resolution of a felony or an offense involving fraud, dishonesty or deceit within 30 days of the disposition or on the next application for appointment and commission, whichever is sooner.

(b) A notary public shall notify the Department of disciplinary action in the nature of a final order taken against the notary's commission by the commissioning authority of another state, territory or country within 30 days of receiving notice of the disciplinary action or on the next application for appointment and commission, whichever is sooner.

(c) A notary public shall notify the Department of a finding against, or admission of liability by, the notary public in any criminal, civil or administrative proceeding within 30 days of conclusion of the legal proceeding or on the next application for appointment and commission, whichever is sooner.

(d) A notary public shall notify the Department of a finding by the Pennsylvania Bar Association or the courts of Pennsylvania or the bar or courts of any other state or nation finding that the notary has engaged in the unauthorized practice of law within 30 days of conclusion of the proceeding or on the next application for appointment and commission, whichever is sooner.

§ 167.124. Conduct providing the basis for disciplinary action.

(a) In addition to the acts and omissions specified by section 323(a) of the Act, the following acts or omissions demonstrate that an individual lacks the honesty, integrity, competence or reliability to act as a notary public:

(1) Notarizing his or her own signature or statement or a spouse's signature or statement.

(2) Notarizing records in blank.

(3) Post-dating or pre-dating notarial acts.

(4) Altering a document after it has been notarized.

(5) Issuing to the order of any State agency or the Commonwealth a personal check without sufficient funds on deposit.

(6) Performing a notarial act within the Commonwealth when the person was not commissioned as a notary public or was otherwise not authorized to perform a notarial act.

(7) Performing a notarial act in another state pursuant to the authority of the notary public's Pennsylvania commission.

(8) Making a representation that the notary public has powers, qualifications, rights or privileges that the notary public does not have.

(9) Use of the term "notario," "notario publico," "notario publica" or any non-English equivalent term in a manner which misrepresents the authority of the notary public.

(10) Engaging in the unauthorized practice of any regulated profession, including but not limited to law.

(11) Endorsing or promoting a product, service, contest or other offering by using the notary public's title or official stamp.

(12) Failure to require the physical presence of an individual making a statement in or executing a signature on a record.

(13) Failure to have personal knowledge or satisfactory evidence of the identity of an individual appearing before the notary.

(14) Executing a notarial certificate that contains a statement known to the notary public to be false.

(15) Using the notary public's official stamp for a purpose other than to perform a notarial act.

(16) Relating to commercial protests as defined in 13 Pa.C.S. §3505(b), failure to identify the negotiable instrument, certify either that presentment has been made or, if not made, the reason why it was not made, and certify that the instrument has been dishonored by nonacceptance or nonpayment, or any combination of the above.

(17) Issuance of a certificate of dishonor of a negotiable instrument

(also known as a protest of commercial paper as defined in 13 Pa.C.S. §3505(b)) that was owned or held for collection by a financial institution, trust company or investment company when the notary public was a party to the commercial paper in an individual capacity.

(18) Issuance of a certificate of dishonor of a negotiable instrument (also known as a protest of commercial paper as defined in 13 Pa.C.S. §3505(b)) of a non-commercial or other record that does not fit the definition of negotiable instrument as defined in 13 Pa.C.S. §3104.

(19) Issuance of a certificate of dishonor of a negotiable instrument (also known as a protest of commercial paper as defined in 13 Pa.C.S. §3505(b)) in a manner not in accordance with 13 Pa.C.S. §3505.

(20) Submission of the following types of records to the Department of State or Secretary of the Commonwealth in reply to correspondence from the Department or other government agency or initiating proceedings through the following record types:

(A) Conditional Acceptance, or a similar record purporting to "conditionally accept" presentment of an official record, and demanding proof of a list of claims in order to fully accept the official record.

(B) Affidavit in Support of Conditional Acceptance, or a similar record purporting to attest to the facts of a record and signed by the same notary public who is attesting.

(C) Notice of Dishonor, or a similar record purporting to give notice that a Conditional Acceptance has not been accepted by the government agency to which it was sent and thereby was dishonored.

(D) Accepted for Value, or similar stamp or certificate purporting to accept for a disclosed or undisclosed value an official record sent to the notary public by the Department of State, Secretary of the Commonwealth or other governmental agency. The certificate claims to establish an amount of money payable or accrued to the signor of the certificate.

(E) Notice of Protest, or a similar record purporting to be a Protest of Commercial Paper that has been dishonored, when said Commercial Paper is not, in fact, a negotiable instrument under Division 3 of Title 13 of the Pennsylvania Consolidated Statutes and subject to the laws stated therein regarding dishonor and protest.

(F) Other records attempting to apply Division 3 of Title 13 of the Pennsylvania Consolidated Statutes to non-negotiable instruments or other records not included in the scope of said chapter.

(G) Other record type purporting to follow the Uniform Commercial Code (UCC) and not related to a filing pursuant to Division 9 of Title 13 of the Pennsylvania Consolidated Statutes.

§ 167.125. Factors considered in disciplinary action

When determining whether to deny an application or take disciplinary action against a notary public, the Department may consider a variety of factors including:

(1) Nature, number and severity of any acts, offenses, official misconduct or crimes under consideration;

(2) Evidence pertaining to the honesty, credibility, truthfulness, and integrity of the applicant or notary public;

(3) Actual or potential monetary or other harm to the general public, group, individual, or client;
(4) History of complaints received by the Department;
(5) Prior disciplinary record or warning from the Department;
(6) Evidence in mitigation;
(7) Evidence in aggravation;
(8) Occupational, vocational, or professional license disciplinary record;
(9) Evidence of rehabilitation, such as reference letters and proof of class attendance;
(10) Criminal record;
(11) Reports from law enforcement agencies;
(12) Willfulness;
(13) Negligence.

§ 167.126. Unauthorized practice of law

(a) In determining whether a notary public has assisted a person in drafting legal records, gave legal advice or is otherwise practicing law (in violation of section 325 of the Act), the Department will take into consideration the factors in Pennsylvania Bar Association Unauthorized Practice of Law (UPL) Committee Formal Opinion 2006-01 or any successor document to that opinion.

(b) Among the acts which constitute the practice of law are the preparation, drafting, or selection or determination of the kind of any legal document, or giving advice in relation to any legal documents or matters.

(c) No person who represents himself in a legal matter shall be considered to have engaged in the unauthorized practice of law.

§ 167.127. Advertising

For the purpose of the statements required by section 325(d) of the Act (relating to representations), the term "prominently" in (d)(ii) means that the entire "I am not an attorney" statement must be in at least 10 point type and the term "prominently" in (d)(iii) means that the entire "I am not an attorney" statement must be displayed in an area open and accessible to the public at the place of performance of the notarial act. ■

About the NNA

Since 1957, the National Notary Association has been committed to serving and educating the nation's Notaries. During that time, the NNA® has become known as the most trusted source of information for and about Notaries and Notary laws, rules and best practices.

The NNA serves Notaries through its Nationalnotary.org website, social media, publications, annual conferences, seminars, online training and the NNA® Hotline, which offers immediate answers to specific questions about notarization.

In addition, the NNA offers the highest quality professional supplies, including official seals and stamps, recordkeeping journals, Notary certificates and Notary bonds.

Though dedicated primarily to educating and assisting Notaries, the NNA supports implementing effective Notary laws and informing the public about the Notary's vital role in today's society.

To learn more about the National Notary Association, visit Nationalnotary.org. ∎

Index

A
Acknowledgments 24–26
Address change 6
Advic 19–20
Affidavits 29–30
Affirmation 26–27
Apostilles.................................. 20–22
Appeal of penalty 52
Application, commission 2–3
Authentication 20–22
Authorized Acts 23

B
Bond, Notary 4–5

C
Certificate, notarial 39–42
Certified Copies of
   Notarial Records 31
Civil lawsuit 52
Copy certification 30–31
Credible identifying witness .. 12–13

D
Depositions 29–30
Disposition of journal 38
Disqualifying interest 17–18
Document dates 36–37

E
Electronic notarization 46–48
Electronic signatures 48
Employee Notaries 8–9
Errors & omissions insurance 4–5
Exam 4

F
Fees 33–34
Foreign-language
   advertisement 19–20
Foreign-language documents 18
Foreign-language signers 18

I
Identification 11–12
Identification documents
   (ID cards).................................. 12
Immigration documents 20–21

J
Journal of notarial acts 35–37
Jurats 27–28
Jurisdiction 6

M
Marriages 50
Motor Vehicle Duties 32

INDEX

N
Name change 6–7
Notarizing for minors 14–15
Notary Oath of Office 5

O
Oaths 26–27

P
Personal appearance 10
Personal knowledge of identity ... 11
Photocopies & faxes 16
Prohibited acts 50
Protests 32

R
Refusal 14
Relatives, notarizing for 17
Resignation 7

S
Signature by mark or stamp ... 13–14
Stamp 43–45
Statement of particulars 39–40
Suspension or revocation
    of appointment 51–52

T
Term of Office 6
Thumbprint 37
Training, mandatory 3

U
Unauthorized practice
    of law 41–42

V
Venue 39
Verifications upon Oath/
    Affirmation (Jurat) 27–28

W
Wills 19
Witnessing/Attesting
    Signature 29–30

NOTES